Quilt
a Gift

Barri Sue Gaudet

Quilt
a Gift

Barri Sue Gaudet

**25 heart-felt projects
from quick to intricate**

David and Charles

A DAVID & CHARLES BOOK

David & Charles is an F+W Media Inc. company
4700 East Galbraith Road
Cincinnati, OH 45236

First published in the UK and US in 2009

ISBN: 978-0-7153-3282-5 paperback
ISBN: 0-7153-3282-1 paperback

Printed in China by RR Donnelley
for David & Charles
Brunel House   Newton Abbot   Devon

Commissioning Editor Jane Trollope
Editor Verity Muir
Project Editor Cathy Joseph
Art Editor Sarah Clark
Senior Designer Jodie Lystor
Production Controller Kelly Smith

Visit our website at www.davidandcharles.co.uk

David & Charles books are available from all good
bookshops; alternatively you can contact our Orderline
on 0870 9908222 or write to us at FREEPOST EX2 110,
D&C Direct, Newton Abbot, TQ12 4ZZ (no stamp required
UK only); US customers call 800-289-0963 and Canadian
customers call 800-840-5220.

Contents

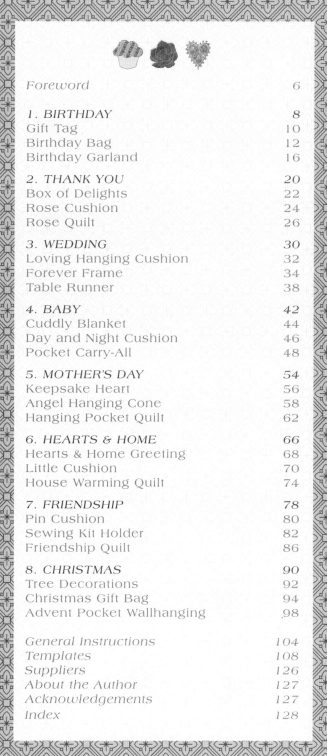

Foreword

Creating a gift by your own hand is a special way to say 'I love you'. Family and friends will appreciate your caring stitches and your handwork will become a treasured keepsake. In this book, you will be sure to find an expression of love and gratitude for many occasions.

The projects contained in these pages are meant for a variety of skill levels. Whether you are new to sewing or more experienced, these unique and sweet remembrances will build your confidence and rejuvenate your love of the simple things in life and the pleasures of giving.

In our fast paced world, finding time to create is becoming more difficult. The projects here will cater for any occasion from a last minute invitation to a well thought-out offering. All you need is an evening to complete the simplest gifts. There are also gifts that may take a week to complete and will become cherished heirlooms. Little tips assist you throughout, from sewing ideas, variations

in design, and ways to complete your gift with a little baked lovely, beautiful flowers, or perhaps a sentimental note.

As soon as you start your projects, you will be pleased to see your confidence grow as the creation comes together. Needlework and its calming essence will have you returning back for other gift-giving occasions throughout the year.

I hope you will enjoy this book and its projects as much as I have loved creating these quilted gifts.

Happy stitching,

Barri Sue Gaudet

Birthday

Everyone loves to celebrate their birthday in style and with these delightful projects you can create birthday décor that will be treasured for years and years.

Make sure that everyone knows where the birthday boy or girl is sitting at the dinner table by marking their place with the little Cupcake mat. They will feel like a VIP on their special and day and make them look forward to dessert even more.

Accessorize your presents with a gift tag or bag to make the act of giving extra special. The Birthday tag can be made quickly and tied to a present as an added personal touch. The Birthday bags are fun to make and can be filled with treats and shared with party guests to make them a present in themselves.

Decorate your party venue by stringing up the Birthday garland and get everyone in a celebratory mood – let the festivities begin!

2½ hour project

Gift Tag

The Gift tag will add that extra personal touch to any gift that you give and the added bonus is that it should only take you 2½ hours, making it a very quick-to-stitch project.

You will need...

- Light colour wool felt: 5in x 4in (12.7cm x 10.2cm)
- Lavender wool felt: 6in x 4in (15.2cm x 10.2cm)
- Tan wool felt: 2in x 3in (5.1cm x 7.6cm)
- White wool felt: 2in x 3in (5.1cm x 7.6cm)
- Green wool felt: 2in x 1in (5.1cm x 2.5cm)
- Yellow wool felt: 1in x 1in (2.5cm x 2.5cm)
- Freezer paper: 8in x 8in (20.3cm x 20.3cm)
- Ribbon: 8in x ¼in (20cm x 6mm)
- Embroidery threads (floss)
- Glue or double-sided fusible webbing 9in x 9in (22.9cm x 22.9cm)
- ¼in (6mm) hole punch

Finished size:
5in x 3½in (12.7cm x 8.9cm)

Templates for this project can be found on page 116

›› Directions

1 Using the template on page 116, trace the background for the tag on to freezer paper and iron to the light coloured piece of wool felt. Cut out the background.

2 Trace the cupcake base, frosting, candle and flame on to freezer paper from the template on page 116. Iron the shapes to the corresponding wool felt colours: the cupcake base to the tan wool felt,

the frosting to the white wool felt, the flame to the yellow wool felt and the candle to green (or the colour of your choice). Cut the shapes out. Following the template and photo, mark out the embroidery lines using a wash-away pen or, if you feel confident, use freehand embroidery. Glue the pieces to the background using the photo (above) for guidance.

3 Using one strand of matching embroidery thread (floss), whipstitch down all the appliqué pieces in place.

4 Remove any tracing lines with a damp sponge and allow to dry if necessary.

5 Using a hole punch, make eleven holes around the scalloped edge of the background. Don't punch the top left hole yet.

6 Glue the completed appliqué top to the 6in x 4in (15.2cm x 10.2cm) piece of lavender wool felt. Punch a hole through the top left corner of all the layers to create a hole for the ribbon. Whipstitch the top to the backing with one strand of matching embroidery thread (floss). Trim the backing so there is ¼in (6mm) showing all around.

7 Fold the ribbon in half and string through the top left opening.

The Cupcake mat is made from a colourful array of wool felts but if you want to adapt the design slightly you could try making it with little scraps of print fabrics in your stash. If you're stuck for a present idea for a special someone the Cupcake mat takes one day to complete so don't leave it right until the last minute.

›› Embroidery

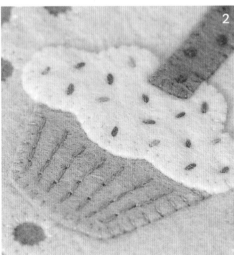

- Backstitch the flame highlights with three strands of orange (1).
- French knot dots on candles with three strands a shade darker than the candle (1).
- Backstitch a wick with two strands of black (1).
- Backstitch sprinkles on the cupcake frosting with three strands of yellow, green, blue and pink (2).
- Backstitch the lines on the cupcake base with three strands of tan (2).

Birthday Bag

Young and old alike will be thrilled with this special little bag, with pieced border, colourful candles and decorative French knots. Allow a day to make it then fill with birthday treats.

You will need...

- Ecru fabric: 9in x 44in (22.9cm x 22.9cm)
- Fourteen blocks from six different coloured fabrics: 1¼in x 1¼in (3.2cm x 3.2cm)
- Lining fabric: two pieces 5¾in x 5in (14.6cm x 12.7cm)
- Medium-weight fusible interfacing: two pieces 5¼in x 4½in (13.3cm x 11.5cm)
- Wool felt in pink, green, blue and yellow: 3in x 3in (7.6cm x 7.6cm)
- Two buttons: ½in (1.3cm)
- Lengths of ribbon in various colours: 12in–24in (30.5cm–61cm)
- Embroidery threads (floss)

Finished size:
5¼in x 4½in (13.3cm x 10.8cm)
Templates for this project can be found on page 118

›› Directions

1 From the ecru fabric, cut a 2¾in x 2in (7cm x 5.1cm) piece for the centre of the bag.

2 Take the fourteen coloured blocks for the inner border and sew two sets of two blocks together in an alternating pattern. Sew these to the two sides of the centre piece and press open. Sew two sets of five blocks together in an alternating pattern and sew to the top and bottom. Press open.

3 For the outer border, cut two 1¼in x 4¼in (3.2cm x 10.8cm) pieces of ecru fabric. Sew to two

sides and press seams open. Cut two 1¼in x 5in pieces of ecru fabric, sew to the remaining sides and press seams open.

4 Take one of your pieces of fusible interfacing. Centre and press the interfacing to the back of the assembled front of the bag ¼in (6mm) from the selvage edge to give the bag added stability.

5 Cut out the appliqué pieces from wool felt and glue or pin in place, using the photo (above) for reference. Using a wash-away pen, draw the positioning of the embroidery

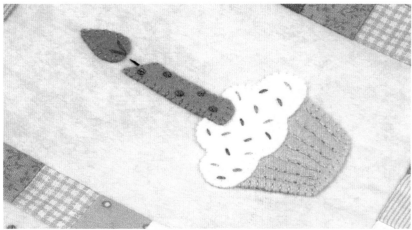

>> TIP

These bags are fun to make because they allow you to make lots of different creative decisions. You don't have to copy the ones that I made, why not try some different options and really make them your own?

>> Embroidery

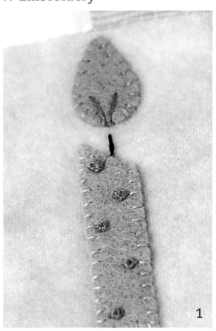

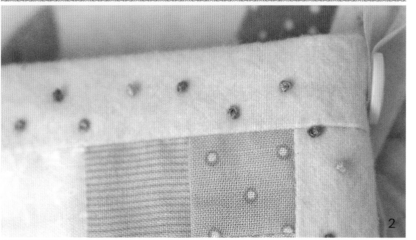

- Backstitch a wick for every candle with two strands of black **(1)**.
- Backstitch a highlight on every flame with three strands of orange **(1)**.
- French knot five dots on every candle with three strands a shade darker than the candle **(1)**.
- French knot dots on the outside border with three strands of green, purple, yellow, pink and blue **(2)**.

embroidery work on to the appliqué pieces following the photo, page 12.

6 Using one strand of matching embroidery thread (floss), whipstitch the wool felt appliqué pieces in place.

7 Stitch the embroidery work following the instructions in the Embroidery box on page 13.

8 Remove any tracing lines with a damp sponge and allow to dry if necessary.

9 Cut a piece of ecru fabric 5¾in x 5in (14.6cm x 12.7cm) for the back of your bag. Take your second piece of fusible interfacing, centre and press to the piece of fabric for the bag back, ¼in (6mm) from the selvage edge.

10 With right sides of the back and front of the bag facing, sew the two pieces together along the sides and bottom only. Trim the edges and clip the corners then turn right sides out and press.

11 Take your two pieces of lining fabric. Right sides together, sew the sides and bottom together, leaving an opening for turning about 3in (7.6cm) along the bottom. Trim the sides and clip the corners. Don't turn the right way out.

12 Put your bag front into your lining so that right sides are together and side seams are matching. Sew the front and lining together ¼in (6mm) from the top edge. Trim this ⅛in (3mm) from the edge. Reach into the opening in the lining and pull it right side out. Press the lining away from the bag front and then whipstitch or topstitch the opening closed. Tuck the lining into the bag and press along the top.

13 Cut two 12in (30.5cm) lengths from your choice of coloured ribbon for the handle. Sew one end of the ribbon to the top left hand corner of the front of the bag and the other to the opposite corner of the back of the bag. Conceal the stitches holding on the ribbon behind two ½in (1.3cm) buttons. Your bag is now complete.

Handles

• A handle that crosses over diagonally from front to back: cut a 9in–12in (23cm–30.5cm) length of ribbon (depending on the size of your bag) and tack each end in place about 1in (2.5cm) from the left side on the front to the opposite side on the back, using two buttons to hide the tacks.

• Handles front and back: cut two 9in–12in (23cm–30.5cm) lengths from three different types of ribbon. Take one piece of each type of ribbon and, making sure that the handles are even, tack each end in place on the front with two buttons, repeat this for the back.

• Side ribbons tied at the top: choose however many ribbons you would like on each side and cut the required number of 15in (38cm) lengths. With all the ribbons together, tack in place with a button at each side at seam.

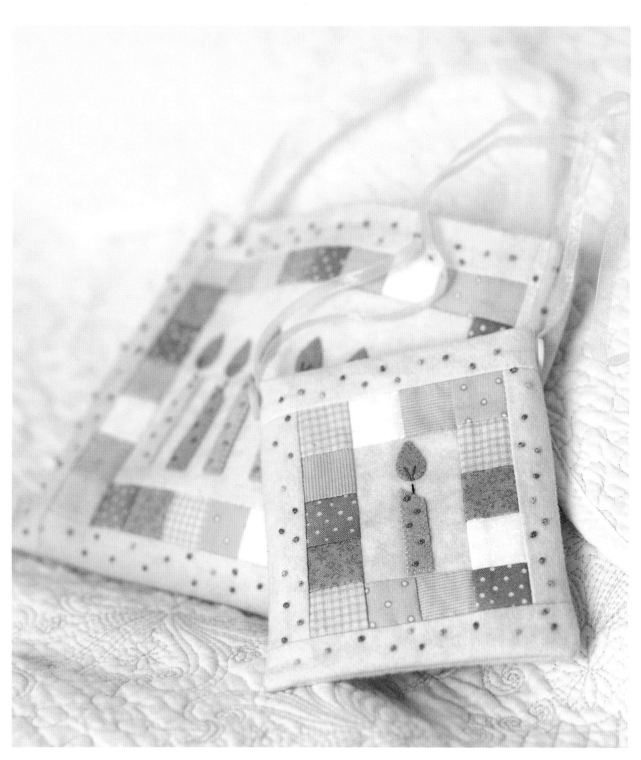

The design of this bag is so versatile, you can easily keep the same dimensions but make the opening at a shorter end and change the appliqué to a single candle. If you prefer, increase the size, following the template on page 118 and add more candles. Each bag will take a day to complete.

Birthday Garland

Welcome the party guests with a gorgeous garland. You can add as many panels as you like and mix and match the appliqué designs to suit the birthday boy or girl. Allow around two hours for each panel.

You will need...

- Ecru fabric: 9in x 5in (22.9cm x 12.7cm) for each panel
- Two strips of very light pink, yellow, blue, or green fabric: 7¼in x 1¼in (18.4cm x 3.2cm) for each panel
- Two strips of very light pink, yellow, blue, or green fabric: 5½in x 1¼in (14cm x 3.2cm) for each panel
- Backing fabric for each panel: 9in x 5½in (22.9cm x 14cm)
- Balloon: 3in x 3in (7.6cm x 7.6cm) three fabrics
- Heart: 6in x 4in (12.2cm x 10.2cm) two pink fabrics
- Cupcake: 4in x 3in (10.2cm x 7.6cm) fabric in tan, white, yellow, orange, and your choice for the candle
- Flower: 4in x 4in (10.2cm x 10.2cm) green, yellow and two other colours.
- Fusible interfacing: 8¾in x 4¾in (22.3cm x 12cm)
- Double-sided fusible webbing
- Rickrack: 30in x ½in (76.2cm x 1.3cm) for each panel
- Two ribbons for each panel: 2½in x ¼in (6.4cm x 6mm)
- Embroidery threads (floss)

Finished size of each panel:
9in x 5½in (22.9cm x 14cm)

Templates for this project can be found on pages 122–123

›› Directions

1 Cut a 4in x 7¼in (10.2cm x 18.4cm) piece of ecru fabric for the centre of each panel of the garland.

2 For the border of each panel, sew the two 7¼ x 1¼in (18.4cm x 3.2cm) strips to the upright sides of the centre of the panel and press open. Then sew the two 5½in x 1¼in (14cm x 3.2cm) strips to the top and bottom and press open.

3 Centre the piece of fusible interfacing on the back of the panel top, leaving ¼in (6mm) of fabric all around. This will stabilize your piece for embroidery work.

4 Stitch the embroidery work for the scalloped border following the instructions in the Embroidery box on page 19.

5 Choose your desired appliqué shape and cut out from the required fabric using the templates provided. Attach the shape to the centre of the panel top using fusible webbing. With a single strand of embroidery thread (floss), whipstitch the appliqué piece in place.

6 Trace embroidery lines for your chosen design using a wash-away pen and stitch following Embroidery directions opposite.

7 Round the corners of your panel top using the trimming guide on the template (page 123). When you've made a few of these you will prpbably be able to do your cutting freehand.

8 Remove the tracing lines with a damp sponge and allow to dry if necessary.

9 Pin or tack (baste) the rickrack to the right side of your panel top. I folded over ¼in (6mm) of rickrack at the beginning of each edge for neatness.

10 Fold the two 2½in (6.4cm) pieces of ribbon in half and pin or tack (baste) where shown on the template to create hanging loops.

11 Take the backing fabric and, with right sides together, sew all around the edges, catching the rickrack and ribbon

loops and leaving an opening for turning. Then trim the edges and turn the correct way out. Whipstitch the opening closed and you've finished a panel for the garland.

12 Make as many panels as you like, choosing colours and appliqué shapes that work well together and then string them all together using a pretty ribbon.

>> TIP

Why not substitute the birthday motifs with Christmas motifs for a festive Christmas garland to decorate the tree or a sweet and welcoming window display? You may change the size of your centres and borders to fit the Christmas appliqué on page 116.

›› Embroidery

- •Running stitch the scallop border on each garland with two strands in a complementary colour (1).
- French knot at each point on the scallop with three strands in a colour of your choice (1).
- Backstitch stems and tendrils on flowers with two strands of light green (2).
- Backstitch balloon strings with two strands of black (3).
- Backstitch a candle wick with two strands of black (4).
- Backstitch ridges on the cupcake base with two strands of tan (5).
- Backstitch sprinkles on cupcake with two strands of pink, yellow, blue and green (5).

Thank You

Sometimes words just don't seem enough to express your thanks to someone but the gift of flowers is always appreciated. Why not go a step further with flowers that last forever, crafted by your hand? Fabric yo-yos, resembling roses in deep reds and pinks are used in these special presents, with appliquéd leaves and embroidered tendrils completing the effect.

For a quick gift, the sweet little fabric box can be filled with chocolates, scented soap or love notes and then kept forever after by the lucky recipient for treasures. Yo-yo roses form a heart on the lovely cushion, symbolizing your deepest gratitude. When time is on your side, the rose quilt will make an elegant wall hanging or a stylish tablemat. Have fun selecting the fabrics in colours you know your friend will love and make it larger or smaller than the pattern, as you please, simply by adding more blocks or taking some away.

 2 hour project

Box of Delights

This little fabric box will take you just a couple of hours to make and can be filled with thank you treats for a quick and creative gift. Once the treats have all gone, it will be so useful for storing odds and ends of jewellery or as a button box.

You will need...

- Light fabric: 8½in x 8½in (21.6cm x 21.6cm)
- Dark fabric: 8½in x 8½in (21.6cm x 21.6cm)
- Fusible interfacing: Two pieces 8½in x 8½in (21.6cm x 21.6cm)
- Four different fabrics with small red prints: seven 2½in x 8in (6.4cm x 20.3cm) pieces
- Green wool felt: 6in x 6in (15.5cm x 15.5cm)
- Freezer paper: 3in x 3in (7.6cm x 7.6cm)
- Ribbon: 40in x ¼in (102cm x 6mm)
- Embroidery threads (floss)
- Fabric glue

Finished size:
2in x 4in x 4in (5.1cm x 10.2cm x 10.2cm)
Templates for this project can be found on page 109

›› Directions

1 Trace the box template on to the 8½in x 8½in (21.6cm x 21.6cm) pieces of light and dark fabric and cut out the shapes.

2 Trace the template twice on to fusible interfacing and cut out. Centre one piece on to the back of the light fabric and one on the back of the dark fabric to strengthen and press into place.

3 To make the yo-yos, take the four different red print fabrics and cut out seven circles (two from fabric one, two from fabric two, two from fabric three and one from fabric four), using the template given.

4 Turn the edge of one circle under by ⅛in (3mm) to the wrong side of the fabric and hand sew a line of running stitches to anchor this seam. Draw up the thread, gathering the fabric to the

middle, and tie off in a knot. Finally, secure the ends of the thread and press to flatten slightly. Repeat with the other six circles to give you seven yo-yos.

5 Trace the leaf template on to freezer paper and cut out fourteen leaves from green wool felt.

6 Following the template, in the middle of the light fabric, glue or pin three yo-yo roses, including the single one from fabric four, and six leaves in place. Whipstitch each rose and leaf in place with one strand of matching embroidery thread (floss).

7 Trace (or freehand embroider) the tendrils around the roses following the Embroidery instructions for the Rose Cushion on page 25.

8 Remove any tracing lines and allow to dry if necessary.

9 Right sides together, sew the backing (dark fabric) to the front, leaving an opening for turning. Trim the seams and clip the corners to points as shown on the template. Turn out the right way around and press. Whipstitch the opening closed.

10 Glue the leaves and yo-yo roses in place at the sides of the box. Leave to dry.

11 Press the sides of the box into position by bending each side at the joint and giving it a good steam. With sewing thread in a colour matching the dark fabric, whipstitch the vertical sides together on the outside only, creating corners.

12 Cut the ribbon into four 10in (25.4cm) lengths and thread one length through each corner using a large crewel needle. Tie each piece of ribbon into a bow for the finishing touch.

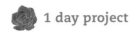

Rose Cushion

Set aside one day for a special token of your appreciation with this beautiful cushion, adorned with yo-yo roses and with two contrasting borders.

You will need...

- Yellow/gold fabric for centre: 7½in x 7½in (19.1cm x 19.1cm)
- Black print fabric for inner border: 2in x 44in (5.1cm x 112cm)
- Large dark print fabric for outer border: 6in x 44in (15.2cm x 112cm)
- Four different red fabrics for roses: 2in x 12in (5cm x 30.5cm)
- Green wool felt: 6in x 6in (15.2cm x 15.2cm)
- Freezer paper: 3in x 3in (7.6cm x 7.6cm)
- Lightweight wadding (batting): 14in x 14in (35.6cm x 35.6cm)
- Backing fabric: 14in x 14in (35.6cm x 35.6cm)
- Stuffing
- Embroidery threads (floss)

Finished size:
12in x 12in (30.5cm x 30.5cm)

Templates for this project can be found on page 108

» Directions

1 To make the first border from the black print fabric, cut two 1¼in x 7½in (3.2cm x 19.1cm) strips for the sides and two 1¼in x 9in (3.2cm x 22.9cm) strips for the top and bottom. Sew the side strips to the yellow/gold centre square and press seams open. Sew the top and bottom strips to the centre square and press seams open.

2 To make the second border from the large dark print fabric, cut two 2½in x 9in (6.4cm x 22.9cm) strips for the sides and two 2½in x 13in (6.4cm x 33cm) strips for the top and bottom. Sew the side strips to the inner border and press seams open. Sew the top and bottom strips to the inner border and press the seams open.

3 To make the yo-yos, cut out twenty-two circles from your red prints using the template. Turn under the edge of one circle by a scant ⅛in (3mm) to the wrong side of the fabric. Hand-sew a line of running stitches

around this edge to anchor the seam. Draw up the thread, gathering the fabric to the middle, and tie off in a knot. Finally, secure the ends of the thread and press to flatten the yo-yo slightly. Repeat with the other twenty-one circles to complete the yo-yos.

4 Trace the leaf template on to freezer paper and cut out thirty-two leaves from the green wool felt.

5 Following the template, pin twenty-four leaves and eighteen yo-yo roses, to form a heart-shape in the centre square of the cushion. Note that the leaves should be placed slightly under the flowers. Pin a rose with two leaves in each corner of the inner border.

6 Trace the tendrils around the roses, referring to the template.

7 Back the cushion top with lightweight wadding (batting) by pinning, tacking (basting) or with spray adhesive to create a quilted effect while stitching. Whipstitch the roses and leaves with one strand of matching embroidery thread (floss). Trim the wadding (batting) all round.

8 Embroider the tendrils around the leaves following the Embroidery instructions, right. Remove any tracing lines and allow to dry if necessary.

9 With right sides together, sew the backing fabric to the cushion front, through the layer of wadding (batting), leaving an opening for turning. Trim the seams and clip the corners. Turn the right side out and stuff the cushion. Whipstitch the opening closed.

>> Embroidery

- Backstitch the tendrils round the roses with three strands of green (1).

1

Rose Quilt

A gesture of kindness will always be remembered with this striking quilt. Allow two to four days when following the design I have given but add or subtract some blocks to the pattern if you choose.

You will need...

- Three different light fabrics for centres and corners: 11in x 44in (27.9cm x 112cm)

- Two different green fabrics: eight pieces 2in x 5in (5cm x 12.7cm)

- Two different red fabrics: eight pieces 2in x 5in (5cm x 12.7cm)

- Ten 2in x 5in (5.1cm x 12.7cm) pieces from three different black fabrics

- Three or four different red small print fabrics for yo-yo roses: 2½in x 24in (6.4cm x 61cm)

- Green wool felt: 12in x 12in (30.5cm x 30.5cm)

- Freezer paper: 5in x 5in (12.7cm x 12.7cm)

- Lightweight wadding (batting): 22in x 22in (55.9cm x 55.9cm)

- Backing fabric: 22in x 22in (55.9cm x 55.9cm)

- Black print fabric for binding: 9in x 44in (22.1cm x 112cm)

- Embroidery threads (floss)

Finished size:
20in x 20in (50.8cm x 50.8cm)

Templates for this project can be found on page 108

›› Directions

1 Before cutting the centres of your patchwork blocks, be sure to reserve enough light fabrics for the corners and setting triangles. You will need three 8½in (21.6cm) squares and two 5½in (14cm) squares reserved for those.

2 Cut thirteen 2in x 5in (5.1cm x 12.7cm) block centres from the three different light fabrics.

3 Take your eight green rectangles and sew matching ones to either side of four block centres. Repeat for the eight red rectangles. Take your ten black rectangles and sew matching ones to either side of five block centres. Press seams open.

4 Following the template and using the photo (above) as a

guide, lay out your blocks to give you the most pleasing arrangement of colours.

5 To make the setting triangles that will form the ends of each row, cut two 8½in (21.6cm) squares from the light fabrics and cut them in half twice diagonally, so you have quarters. For the corner triangles, cut two 5½in (14cm) squares in half diagonally.

6 Sew the blocks and side setting triangles into rows and press. Sew the rows together to form the quilt top and press. Sew on the corner triangles and press. Trim the quilt top to 20in (50cm) square.

7 To make the yo-yos, cut out twenty-five circles using the template. Turn under the edge of one circle by a scant 1/8in (3mm) to the wrong side of the fabric. Hand-sew a line of running stitches around this to anchor the seam. Draw up the thread, gathering the fabric to the middle, and tie off in a knot. Finally, secure the ends of the thread and press to flatten the yo-yo slightly.

8 Trace the leaf template on to freezer paper and cut out sixty-two leaves from the green wool felt.

9 On the light centres of the blocks, trace (or freehand embroider) lines for stems and tendrils, following the template and photo (page 28). Glue or pin the yo-yo flowers and leaves in place then secure with whipstitch, using

one strand of matching embroidery thread (floss). On each side and corner triangle, glue or pin the leaves and flowers in place, trace (or freehand embroider) lines for the tendrils and then secure the flowers with whipstitch.

10 Back the quilt with lightweight wadding (batting) by pinning, tacking (basting) or with spray adhesive to create a quilted effect while stitching.

11 Embroider following Embroidery directions, right. Remove any tracing lines and allow to dry if necessary.

12 Back the quilt with your backing fabric, quilt as desired and bind to finish, following the binding instructions on page 105.

>> Embroidery

- Backstitch the tendrils round the roses with three strands of green **(1)**.
- Backstitch the flower stems with three strands of green **(2)**.

Wedding

A forthcoming wedding among friends
or family is such a special occasion that
it deserves the personal touch of a gift
you have lovingly made to wish the
couple a long and happy future together.
Soft, pastel colours, delicate seed bead
clusters, connected hearts, and lovebirds
are a visual celebration of wedding day
bliss. Your creations are certain to become
heirlooms to remember that joy.

Patchwork blocks are appliquéd with
symbols of love and embroidered in a
romantic table runner while two hearts,
pieced together, make a sweet little pillow
reminding the couple of their love and
your hopes for them. A picture frame is
a practical item that takes on so much
more meaning with a delightful border,
decorated with hearts and flowers. Pop
a photo of the couple, or perhaps their
wedding invitation, behind the ribbons as
a unique memento.

Loving Hanging Cushion

Taking just two or three hours this little cushion is a quick and easy project that will look so sweet hanging in the couple's bedroom. Embroidering their initials on their hearts would make a lovely finishing touch.

You will need...

- Blue fabric for centre: 4½in x 4½in (11.4cm x 11.4cm)
- Off-white fabric for borders: 4½in x 43in (11.4cm x 109.2cm)
- Off-white fabric for cushion back: 7in x 7in (17.8cm x 17.8cm)
- Pink wool felt: 5in x 5in (12.7cm x 12.7cm)
- Freezer paper: 3in x 3in (7.6cm x 7.6cm)
- Lightweight wadding (batting): 7in x 7in (17.8cm x 17.8cm)
- Off-white ribbon: 12in (30.5cm) of ¼in (6mm)
- Small packs of white and pink seed beads
- Two to three handfuls of stuffing
- Embroidery threads (floss)

Finished size:
6in x 6in (15.2cm x 15.2cm)

Templates for this project can be found on page 115

›› Directions

1 To make the off-white border for the blue fabric centre, cut two sides, each 1½in x 4½in (3.8cm x 11.4cm). Sew in place and press seams open. Cut the top and bottom, each 1½in x 6½in (3.8cm x 16.5cm), sew in place and press seams open.

2 Trace the template on to freezer paper and cut out two hearts from the pink wool felt. Glue or pin in place on the blue centre, following the template and photo (above). Using one strand of matching embroidery thread (floss), whipstitch the appliqué pieces.

3 Back the cushion front with lightweight wadding (batting) by pinning, tacking (basting) or with spray adhesive, to create a quilted effect while stitching.

4 Trace the embroidery lines of vines and leaves from the

template using freezer paper. Stitch following Embroidery directions (right). Remove the tracing lines and allow to dry if necessary.

5 With a single strand of white embroidery thread (floss), sew clusters of white seed beads to the vine, following the template and photo. With pink stranded cotton (floss), sew pink seed beads all around the outside of the hearts, as indicated on the template and photo (right).

6 Pin or tack (baste) the ribbon to the cushion front where shown on the template.

7 Take your piece of off-white fabric for the back of the cushion and right sides together, sew the back to the front leaving an opening for turning. Clip the corners. Turn the right way round and stuff. Whipstitch the opening closed.

>> Embroidery

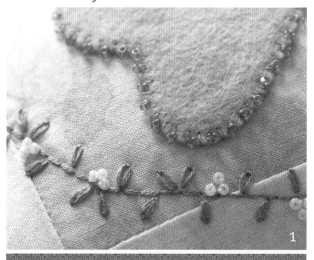

1

- Backstitch the vines with two strands of green **(1)**.
- Lazy daisy stitch the leaves with two strands of green **(1)**.

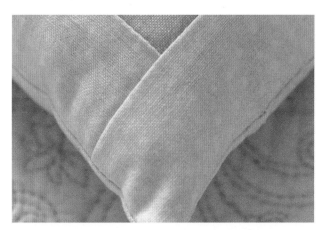

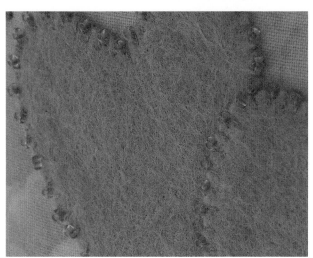

Forever Frame

With a vine and its seed bead flowers intertwining the border, pairs of appliqué hearts and ribbons to hold a photo in place, this frame is the perfect romantic gift to celebrate a wonderful day. Allow one to two days to complete.

You will need...

- Large print fabric for centre: 5in x 7in (12.7cm x 17.8cm)
- Small print fabric for second border: 4½in x 8in (11.4cm x 20cm)
- Pale pink fabric: 4½in x 44in (11.4cm x 112cm)
- Off-white ribbon: 12in x ¼in (30.5cm x 6mm)
- Pink wool felt: 6in x 6in (15.2cm x 15.2cm)
- Freezer paper: 3in x 3in (7.6cm x 7.6cm)
- Lightweight wadding (batting): 10in x 14in (25.4cm x 35.6cm)
- Small pack of white seed beads
- Picture frame: 8in x 10in (20.3cm x 25.4cm)
- Embroidery threads (floss)
- Tape

Finished size:

8in x 10in (20.3cm x 25.4cm)

Templates for this project can be found on page 113

❯❯ Directions

1 Take your 7in x 5in (17.9cm x 12.7cm) large print fabric. Cut 12in (30cm) ribbon into four equal lengths and, following the template, tack (baste) or glue the ribbon in place on the corners of the fabric. Make sure the ribbon extends over the selvage so it will be caught in the border seam.

2 To make the first border, cut two 7in x 1in (17.8cm x 2.5cm) strips from the pale pink fabric. Sew to either side of the centre piece and

> ❯❯ **TIP**
>
> *I have found that frames are ½in (1.3cm) smaller inside than their stated dimensions. So an 8in x 10in (20.3cm x 25.4cm) frame has a 4½in x 9½in (11.4cm x 24.1cm) inside opening. The instructions here accommodate this sizing. If you have a larger or smaller frame, simply lengthen or shorten the borders to fit.*

press open. Cut two 6in x 1in (15.2cm x 2.5cm) strips from the pale pink fabric, sew to the top and bottom of the centre and press seams open.

3 For the second border, cut two ¾in x 8in (1.9cm x 20.3cm) strips from the small print fabric. Sew to the sides of the first border and press open. Cut two ¾in x 6½in (1.9cm x 16.5cm) strips from the fabric and sew to the top and bottom of the first border. Press seams open.

4 The third border is large enough to stretch over the insert of the frame. Cut two 2½in x 8½in (6.4cm x 21.6cm) strips from the pale pink fabric. Sew to the sides of the second border and press seams open. Cut two 2½in x 10½in (6.4cm x 26.7cm) strips from the fabric and sew to the top and bottom of the second border.

5 Cut out eight hearts from wool felt and whipstitch in place following the template and photos.

6 Using the template, trace embroidery lines of vines (or embroider freehand).

7 Back the piece with wadding (batting) by pinning, tacking (basting) or with spray adhesive, to create a quilted effect while stitching.

8 Embroider the vines and leaves following the Embroidery instructions, opposite. Remove tracing lines, allow to dry if necessary then press.

10 With a single strand of embroidery thread (floss), sew seed beads in clusters of three to represent flowers, as shown on the template and in the photo, below.

11 Using the glass insert that came with your frame, centre and stretch your top to the glass. Hold in place with tape. Put it into the frame to check the positioning, then place the backing that came with the frame (or cut your own) over it. Tuck a photo or the wedding invitation into the ribbon corners to finish.

›› Embroidery

- Backstitch the vines with two strands of green.
- Lazy daisy stitch the leaves on the vines with two strands of green.

Table Runner

So pretty in pink, this runner will take pride of place on the couple's dining table. With the patchwork, appliqué and embroidery details it takes a little time to make, so start well in advance of the wedding and allow yourself one week to finish.

You will need...

- Three pink fabrics for centre squares: 9in x 44in (23cm x 112cm)
- Pink print fabric for block corner squares: 4½in x 44in (11.4cm x 112cm)
- Pink/white print for block borders: 4½in x 44in (11.4cm x 112cm)
- Off-white fabric for first border, sashing and third border: 18in x 44in (46cmcm x 112cm)
- Plain pink fabric for second border: 4½in x 44in (11.4cm x 112cm)
- White wool felt: 10in x 10in (25.5cm x 25.5cm)
- Yellow wool felt: 2in x 2in (5cm x 5cm)
- Pink wool felt: 10in x 10in (25.5cm x 25.5cm)
- Freezer paper: 10in x 10in (25.5cm x 25.5cm)
- Lightweight wadding (batting): 17in x 43in (43.2cm x 109.2cm)
- Backing fabric: 17in x 43in (43.2cm x 109.2cm)
- Pink fabric for bias binding: ¾in x 43in (2cm x 109.2cm)
- Small pack of white seed beads
- Cutting mat and rotary cutter
- Embroidery threads (floss)

Finished size:
14in x 40in (35.6cm x 101.5cm)

Templates for this project can be found on pages 114–115

» Directions

1 To make the blocks, first cut out five 4½in x 4½in (11.4cm x 11.4cm) squares from the three pink fabrics. From the pink/white print fabric, cut ten 1½in x 4½in (3.2cm x 3.2cm) rectangles and sew to the sides of each square. Press seams open.

2 Cut one strip 4½in x 17in (11.4cm x 43.1cm) from pink/white print fabric. Cut two strips 1½in x 17in (3.2cm x 43.1cm) from pink print fabric for the corner squares. Sew a pink print strip to either side of the 4½in (11.4cm) strip along the 17in length. Press open. Lay the joined strips horizontally on a cutting mat and cut into 1½in (3.2cm) strips with a rotary cutter. Sew to the top and bottom of each block and press seams open. The five blocks should each measure 6½in (16.5cm) square.

3 For the sashing (in between the blocks) cut four 6½in x 1¼in (16.5cm x 3.2cm) strips from off-white fabric. Sew the blocks together with one of these strips between each block, ends left free. You should now have a length of five blocks in a row.

4 For the first border, cut two strips 1¼in x 33½in (3.2cm x 85.1cm) from the off-white fabric. Sew to the top and bottom and press open. Cut two strips 1¼in x 8in (3.2cm x 20.3cm), sew to either end and press seams open.

5 For the second border, cut two strips 1in x 35in (2.5 x 22.9cm) from plain pink fabric. Sew to the top and bottom of the first border and press open. Cut two strips 1in x 9in (2.5 x 88.9cm), sew to either end and press seams open.

6 For the third border, cut two strips 4in x 36in (10.2cm x 91.4cm) from off-white fabric. Sew to the top and bottom of the second border and press open. Finally, cut two strips 4in x 16in (10.2cm x 40.6cm), sew to either end and press seams open.

7 Trace the templates for the dove, beak, wings, small hearts and large hearts on to freezer paper. Cut out from corresponding wool felt, following the photos (opposite).

8 Using the templates for guidance, glue or pin all the appliqué pieces in place. With a single strand of matching embroidery thread (floss), whipstitch in place.

9 Trace embroidery lines.

10 Back the piece with lightweight wadding (batting) by pinning, tacking (basting) or with spray adhesive, to create a quilted effect while stitching.

11 Embroider according to the Embroidery instructions (opposite). Remove tracing lines, allow to dry if necessary then press.

12 With a single strand of white embroidery thread (floss), sew seed bead clusters to the vines, where shown on the template.

13 Following the template, cut a scallop edge all around your runner.

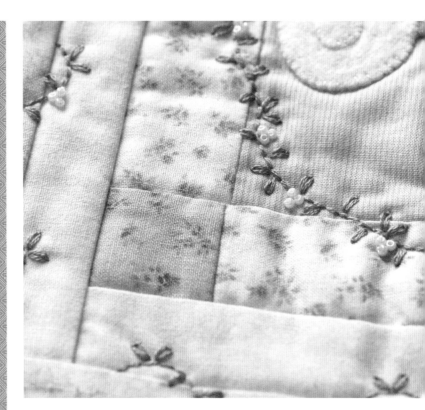

14 Back the runner with backing fabric and bind with binding cut on the bias (see binding instructions page 105).

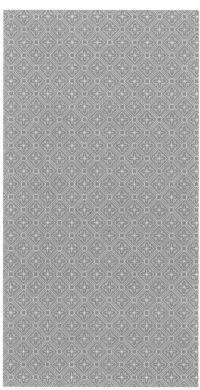

>> Embroidery

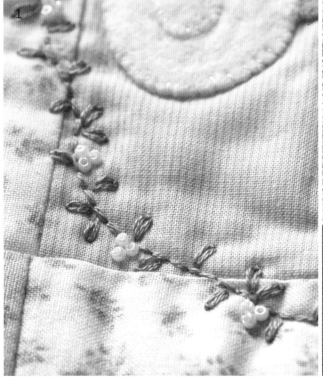

- French knot the dove's eyes with two strands of black **(1)**.
- Backstitch the vines with two strands of green **(2)**.
- Lazy daisy stitch the leaves with two strands of green **(2)**.

Baby

The excitement of a new baby always brings coos of delight at the perfect little being brought into the world. Tiny clothes will soon be outgrown but these three gifts will stand the test of time. Lots of colourful fabrics and the ease of wool felts make them simple and charming. They will look great in the nursery but have a practical use, too, which the proud parents will appreciate.

The cuddly blanket is so quick to make and you can easily change the look by picking any one of the appliqué motifs that you will find on the pattern pages. A very special pillow for the cot offers a cheery face for both night and day, while the delightful pocket carry-all is a creative way to keep the nursery tidy.

These gifts are ideal for a boy or a girl so you can prepare them well ahead of the due date and have a wonderful surprise to offer the new family on your first visit.

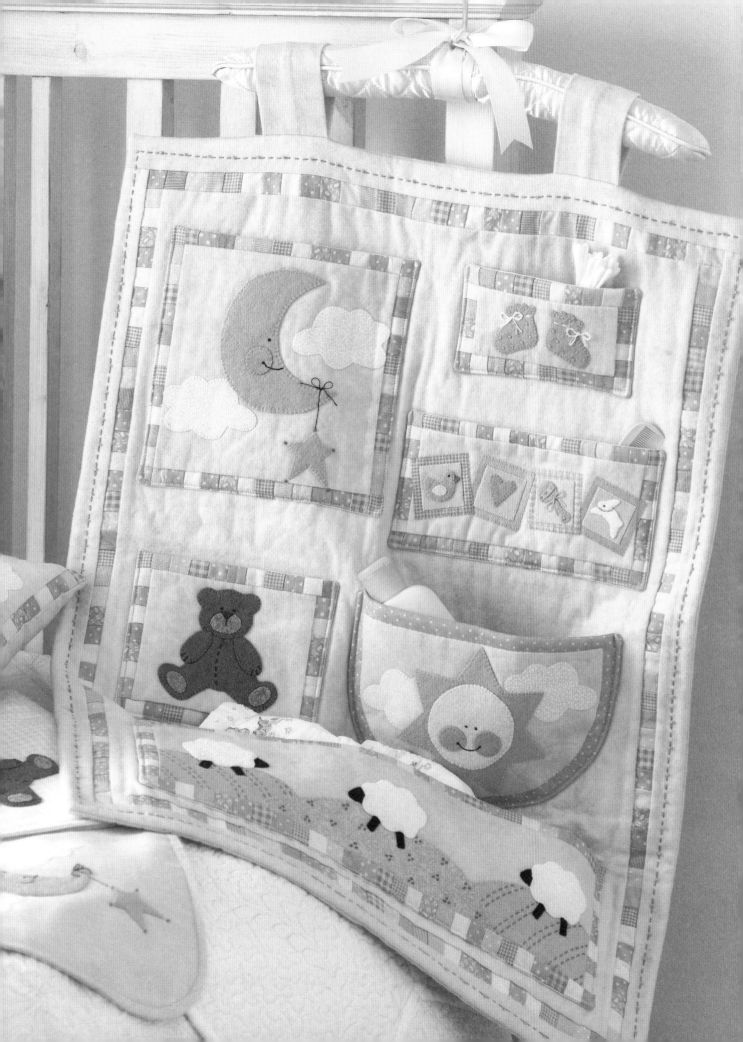

Cuddly Blanket

You can never have too many blankets for a baby and this one, in soft flannel, will be wonderful to snuggle up with for an afternoon nap in the cot, or to stay cozy for a walk in the park. With just a simple appliqué you can make it in three hours.

You will need...

- Two flannels in the same or complementary colours: 36in x 36in (91.5cm x 91.5cm)

- Brown wool felt: 8in x 8in (20cm x 20cm)

- Tan wool felt: 3in x 3in (7.5cm x 7.5cm)

- Freezer paper: 8in x 8in (20cm x 20cm)

- Embroidery thread (floss)

Finished size:
36in x 36in (91.5cm x 91.5cm)

Templates for this project can be found on pages 120–121

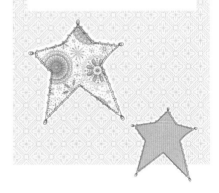

» Directions

1 Round the corners of the two flannel pieces using the template on page 120.

2 Using the templates, trace the bear appliqué pieces on to freezer paper, iron on to the corresponding wool felt and cut out.

3 Trace the embroidery lines (or freehand embroider).

4 Glue or pin the appliqué pieces to one flannel piece at the rounded corner, about 2in (5cm) from the edge.

5 Appliqué the bear pieces using primitive whipstitch.

6 Embroider following Embroidery directions (below). Remove any tracing lines and allow to dry if necessary.

7 Right sides together, sew the two flannel pieces together all around leaving an opening for turning. Trim the edges and slipstitch the opening closed.

8 Topstitch ¼ in (6mm) from the edge all around.

>> Embroidery

- Satin stitch the bear's nose with three strands of dark brown **(1)**.
- French knot the eyes with three strands of black **(1)**.
- Backstitch or running stitch the seam lines and claws with three strands of dark brown **(2)**.

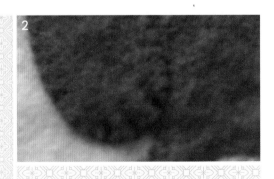

 **1 day project**

Day and Night Cushion

This double-sided cushion is like giving two gifts in one. Sunny-side up it will brighten baby's room during the daytime while the jolly moon will make bedtime a pleasure and ensure that the sweetest of dreams will follow. Set aside a day to complete the project.

You will need...

- Two pieces of off-white fabric: 7in x 8½in (18cm x 21.5cm)
- Strips of six different coloured fabrics: 4in x 15in (10cm x 38cm)
- Yellow wool felt: 5in x 10in (13cm x 25.5cm)
- Pink, blue, light yellow wool felt: 3in x 3in (7.5cm x 7.5cm)
- Freezer paper: 12in x 12in (30cm x 30cm)
- Two white-on-white prints: 5in x 4in (13cm x 10cm)
- Double-sided fusible webbing: 5in x 4in (13cm x 10cm)
- Two pieces of lightweight wadding (batting): 8in x 10in (20cm x 25.5cm)
- Small pack of stuffing
- Cutting mat and rotary cutter
- Embroidery thread

Finished size:
7½in x 9in (19cm x 23cm)

Templates for this project can be found on page 120

›› Directions

1 Cut the colour strips for the border 1in (2.5cm) wide. To strip-piece these, sew your strips together along the 15in (38cm) length, alternating colours. Sew as many as you need to create a 7in (18cm) width (about 14). Press these flat.

2 Lay your work on your cutting mat so that the seams are horizontal and cut four 1in (2.5cm) strips from this. Sew these to the sides of your 7in x 8½in (18cm x 21.5cm) off-white centres. Press open. Now add more strips for your top and bottom borders (about 18).

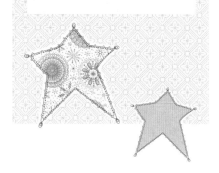

Cut four 1in (2.5cm) strips horizontally again. Sew to the top and bottom of the centres and press open.

3 Trace the cloud templates on to double-sided fusible webbing and fuse the four clouds on to the two different white-on-white fabrics. Fuse these on to the cushion fronts, referring to the templates and photos for positioning.

4 From the templates, use freezer paper to trace and cut out the moon and sun appliqué pieces from the wool felts. Glue in place on the cushion fronts – the moon pieces on one and the sun on the other.

5 Trace embroidery lines (or freehand embroider).

6 Back each front with lightweight batting (wadding) by pinning, tacking (basting) or with spray adhesive to create a quilted effect while stitching.

7 Using a primitive whipstitch and a single strand of matching embroidery thread (floss), whipstitch all the appliqué to each cushion top.

8 Embroider following Embroidery directions (below). Remove any tracing lines and allow to dry if necessary.

9 Right sides together, sew the two tops together leaving an opening for turning. Turn the right way round and stuff. Whipstitch the opening closed.

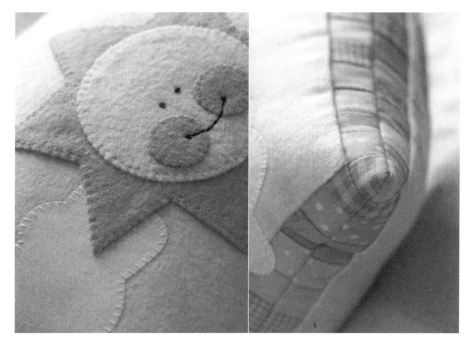

›› Embroidery

- Backstitch smiles on the moon and the sun with two strands of black (1).
- French knot eyes on the moon and the sun with two strands of black (1).
- Backstitch a string from the moon to the star with one strand of black. Tie a bow at the top of your string with one strand of black and secure with glue (2).
- French knot a dot at the points of the star with two strands of blue (2).

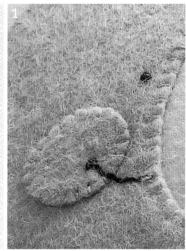
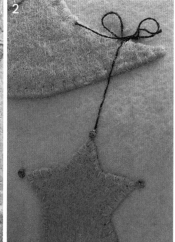

Pocket Carry-All

This delightful hanging space-saver is as practical as it is cute, with plenty of pockets to keep all those essential bits and pieces tidy in the nursery. As baby grows, it can be used for little toys. There is quite a bit of detail involved so allow seven to 10 days.

You will need...

- Ecru fabric for background, borders, tabs and pocket centres: 36in x 44in (91.5cm x 112cm)
- Strips of yellow, blue, purple, green, white, and pink fabric for pieced border: 4in x 44in (10cm x 112cm)
- Blue fabric: two pieces 10in x 7in (25.5cm x 18cm) for scalloped pocket
- Light yellow and yellow wool felt: 5in x 10in (13cm x 25.5cm)
- White and brown wool felt: 6in x 6in (15.5cm x 15.5cm)
- Blue and pink wool felt: 4in x 4in (10cm x 10cm)
- Black, tan, and orange wool felt: 2in x 2in (5cm x 5cm)
- Freezer paper: 24in (61cm)
- Scraps of fabric prints: two light greens, two whites, off-white, pink and blue
- Double-sided fusible webbing: 10in (25.5cm)
- Muslin: 18in x 44in (46cm x 112cm)
- Lightweight wadding (batting): 36in x 45in (91.5cm x 111.8cm)
- Backing fabric: 22in x 29in (56cm x 73.6cm)
- Pretty hanger
- Embroidery thread (floss)

Finished size:

20in x 30in (50cm x 50cm) with hanger

Templates for this project can be found on pages 120–122

›› Directions

1 Cut all pocket centres from ecru fabric:
  - A: 7in x 7in (18cm x 18cm)
- B: 2½in x 5in (6.5cm x 13cm)
- C: 3½in x 7½ (9 x 19cm)
- D: 4½in x 5½in (11.5cm x 14cm)
- F: 4½in x 15in (11.5cm x 38cm)

- E: (scallop) cut following the template. Add ¼in (6mm) all around for turned under appliqué, cut out to given size to fuse appliqué. Cut out the blue background piece adding ¼in (6mm) to the template given. This piece will have a lining and need to be sewn.

2 Using double-sided fusible webbing (see General instructions page 104), trace and cut out the land pieces from green fabric scraps and fuse on to the bottom pocket F so the edges will catch in the seam when you sew on the border. Refer to the template to see where the land pieces extend.

3 Attach the ecru scallop pocket E to the blue background piece by sewing or fusing with double-sided fusible webbing.

4 To make the strip-pieced borders for the pockets, first cut your array of colour strips 1in (2.5cm) wide. Sew these together along the length, adding as many as you need to create a length for each pocket side. Press flat. Lay your joined strips on your cutting board so that the seams are horizontal and cut 1in (2.5cm) strips from this. Sew to the sides of your off-white centres, trimming to fit. Press open. Now join

more strips together for your top and bottom borders. Cut again, horizontally, 1in (2.5cm) wide. Sew to the top and bottom of the pockets, again trimming to fit, and press open.

5 Cut out the remaining appliqué pieces from your fabric scraps.

Use double-sided fusible webbing to apply the clouds in pockets A and E and the blocks in pocket C.

6 Use freezer paper to trace and cut out the wool felt appliqué pieces following the templates and the photo (page 49).

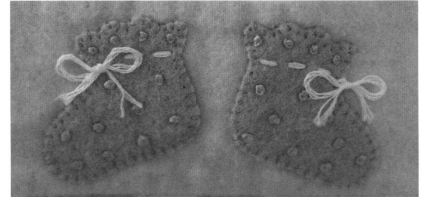

7 Trace embroidery lines with a wash-away pen.

8 Back each pocket with lightweight wadding (batting) by pinning, tacking (basting) or with spray adhesive to create a quilted effect while stitching.

9 Using a primitive whipstitch and a single strand of matching embroidery thread (floss), whipstitch all appliqué (wool felt and fabric).

10 Embroider following Embroidery directions (page 52). Remove any tracing lines and allow to dry if necessary.

11 Right sides together, sew a muslin lining to each pocket except for E, which has a blue fabric lining, leaving an opening for turning. Clip the corners and trim seams. Whipstitch the openings closed. Set the pockets aside for now.

12 Cut a 17½in x 24in (45cm x 61cm) background for the carry-all from the ecru fabric.

13 Use your 1in (2.5cm) strips again for the first, strip-pieced, border and follow the instructions in step 4. The sides need to be 1in x 24in (2.5cm x 61cm). Sew these on first and press seams open. The top and bottom borders are 1in x 18½in (2.5cm x 47cm). Sew these in place and press seams open.

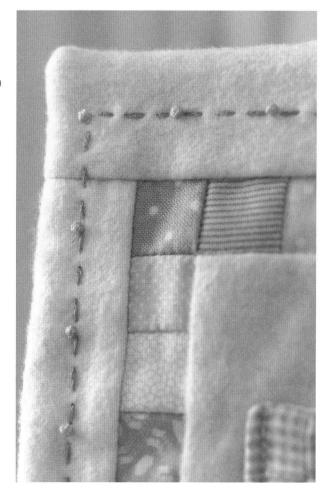

14 For the second, ecru border, cut two 1½in x 25in (4cm x 63.5cm) strips, sew to the sides and press open. Cut two 1½in x 20½in (4cm x 52cm) strips, sew to the top and bottom and press seams open.

15 Trace embroidery lines on the second border and then back the piece with wadding (batting) by pinning, tacking (basting) or with spray adhesive.

16 Stitch the embroidery following Embroidery directions (right).

17 To make the tabs for hanging, cut two 4½in x 7in (11.5cm x 18cm) from off-white fabric. Take one piece and, right sides together, fold in half along the 7in (18cm) edge. Sew along the length, turn and press. Fold in half again, matching the raw edges. Pin or tack (baste) in place, matching the raw edge along the top. Repeat for the other tab. Each tab should be approximately 4½in (11.5cm) from the outside corner and 3½in (9cm) from the centre.

19 Place this finished piece on your backing fabric, right sides together, and sew all around leaving an opening for turning. Clip corners and trim edges. Turn through and whipstitch the opening closed.

20 Pin the pockets in place following the pattern (page 121). Topstitch through all the layers the sides and bottom of each pocket, ⅛in (3mm) from the edge.

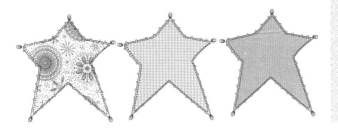

>> Embroidery

- Backstitch smiles on the moon and sun with two strands of black **(1)**.
- French knot eyes on the moon, duck, bunny and bear with two strands of black **(2)**.
- Backstitch a string from the moon to the star with one strand of black. Tie a bow at the top of your string with one strand of black and secure with glue **(3)**.
- French knot a dot at the points of the star with two strands of blue.
- French knot dots on the booties with three strands of yellow **(4)**.
- Running stitch along the top of the booties with three strands of white, tie a bow on each booty and secure with glue **(4)**.
- French knot dots on the sheep with three strands of white **(5)**.
- Backstitch a collar on the bunny with three strands of pink **(6)**.
- French knot a dot on the bottom of the rattle with three strands of yellow, tie a bow on the rattle and secure with glue.
- French knot dots on the rattle stripe with three strands of green **(7)**.
- French knot dots on the middle hill of the sheep pocket with three strands of green.
- Running stitch furrows on the right and left hill of the sheep block with three strands of green **(8)**.
- Running stitch and backstitch the seam and claws of the bear with three strands of dark brown.
- Satin stitch the bear's nose with three strands of dark brown.
- Running stitch around the border with two strands of blue.
- French knot dots around the border with three strands of yellow.

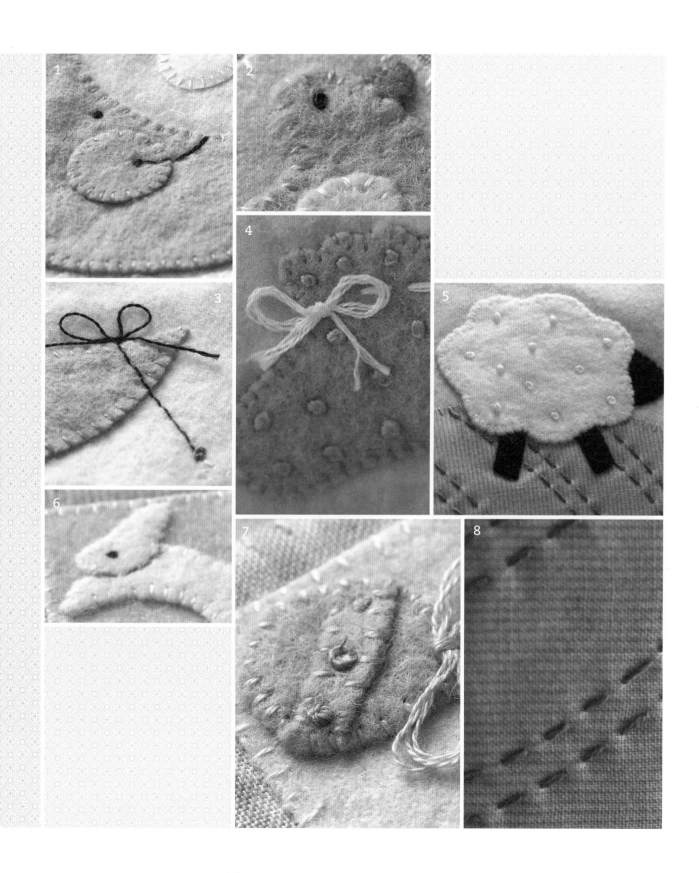

Mother's Day

Mothers are our guides, protectors and friends. They are a shoulder to cry on when things go wrong and the first to share in our joy and success. Let your mother know what an angel she is to you with these heavenly handicrafts.

Three little items to hang in the home, they are all so pretty by themselves but you can make them even more special by filling with gifts. An angelic wall hanging has an appliquéd heart pocket at its centre – perfect for a display of spring flowers. The fabric cone with scallop edge and dear little floating angel can be filled with any manner of treats, from luxury chocolates to a favourite scent. Small but perfectly formed, the keepsake heart also has a little pocket for a single bloom, a loving note or a fond photo.

Keepsake Heart

Made from wool felts and ribbon, this is a beautiful and easy keepsake that will take just two to three hours. The pocket could hold a very special note, a photo or a poem along with a single flower peeping out from the top.

You will need...

- Ecru wool felt: 4in x 4in (10cm x 10cm)
- Pink wool felt: 5in x 9in (13cm x 23cm)
- Green wool felt: 3in x 2in (7.5cm x 5cm)
- Freezer paper: 8in x 8in (20cm x 20cm)
- Off-white ribbon: 40in (101.5cm) of ¼in (6mm) and 8in of ⅛in (3mm).
- Embroidery threads (floss)

Finished size:
3½in x 4in (9cm x 10cm)

Templates for this project can be found on pages 109

» Directions

1 Trace the large and small hearts, flowers and leaves on to freezer paper. Press the freezer paper templates to corresponding wool felt and cut out one small ecru heart, two larger pink hearts, three pink flowers and eight leaves.

2 Cut three 2½in lengths of ⅛in (3mm) wide off-white ribbon. Cut three 1¼in (3.25cm) lengths of ¼in (6mm) wide off-white ribbon. Fold the narrower ribbons in half to create loops. Pin or tack (baste) the ribbon in place on the small heart, following the pattern and photo (above), with the loops on top of the wider lengths.

3 Following the pattern and photo, glue or pin the leaves and flowers in place. Whipstitch round the flowers with a single strand of matching embroidery thread (floss), catching the leaves and ribbon in the stitches. Do not sew the leaves down completely.

Embroider the flowers according to Embroidery instructions below.

4 Using one strand of matching embroidery thread (floss), whipstitch the finished small heart to one of the larger pink hearts.

5 Cut two lengths of ¼in (6mm) off-white ribbon 14in (35.5cm) long. Using three strands of pink embroidery thread (floss), sew the pink hearts with a blanket stitch, catching a length of ribbon at each side where shown on the pattern and photo (right). Leave an opening at the top for a pocket. Tie a bow at the ends of the ribbon to finish.

›› Embroidery

- French knot a centre for each flower with three strands of yellow (1).

1

Angel Hanging Cone

Delicate flowers border the scallop edge and the dearest of angels brightens this elegant hanging holder. Allow a day to make it and then fill with your mother's favourite treats or flowers to indulge her on Mother's Day.

You will need...

- Light green fabric: 13in x 15in (33cm x 38cm)
- Fabric for lining: 13in x 15in (33cm x 38cm)
- Off-white fabric: 5in x 15in (13cm x 38cm)
- Fusible interfacing: 13in x 15in (33cm x 38cm)
- Pink wool felt: 6in x 6in (15.5cm x 15.5cm)
- Off-white, yellow and green wool felt: 4in x 4in (10cm x 10cm)
- Peach wool felt: 3in x 3in (7.5cm x 7.5cm)
- Freezer paper: 8in x 8in (20cm x 20cm)
- Two wired ribbons: 15in x 1in (38cm x 2.5cm).
- Double-sided fusible webbing (optional): 5in x 15in (13cm x 38cm)
- Embroidery threads (floss)

Finished size:
11in (28cm) tall with 14in (35.5cm) circle opening

Templates for this project can be found on pages 109–110

›› Directions

1 Using the template, trace the shape of the cone to light green fabric. Flip the template at the centre line to create a whole triangle approximately 13½in (34.4cm) across with a curved top. Back this with a piece of fusible interfacing cut ¼in (6mm) smaller. Centre to the back of the light green piece and press. This will stabilize your cone.

2 Trace the shape of the cone to your lining fabric and cut out the same as your light green piece. Set this lining piece aside for now.

3 For turned appliqué, add ¼in (6mm) to the scallop top template along the scallop edge. Cut one scallop top from the off-white fabric, flipping the template as for the cone shape. Turn under the seam of the scallop edge and press. Leave the top curve as it is and match to the top edge of the light green front piece. Whipstitch in place along the scallop edge. The top and sides will be caught in the seams.

4 Trace the appliqué pieces on to freezer paper. Press the freezer paper templates to wool felt and cut out (see General instructions page 106). Following the template, glue or pin in place on the green fabric. Be sure to note where some pieces overlap with others, for example the leaves and dress.

5 Trace (or freehand embroider) the lines for eyes and the flower centres to the wool felt pieces. Trace the stem to the background piece. Whipstitch the appliqué pieces using one strand of matching embroidery thread (floss). Leave the leaves free, just holding them in place with the whipstich on the flowers. Note: leave one flower off near the side seam.

> **›› TIP**
> *Instead of turned applique in step 3, trace the scallop top to double-sided fusible webbing and press to the back of the off-white fabric. Cut out along the line indicated in the template, adding ¼in (6mm) along the curved top and sides to match the light green front piece. Fuse in place.*

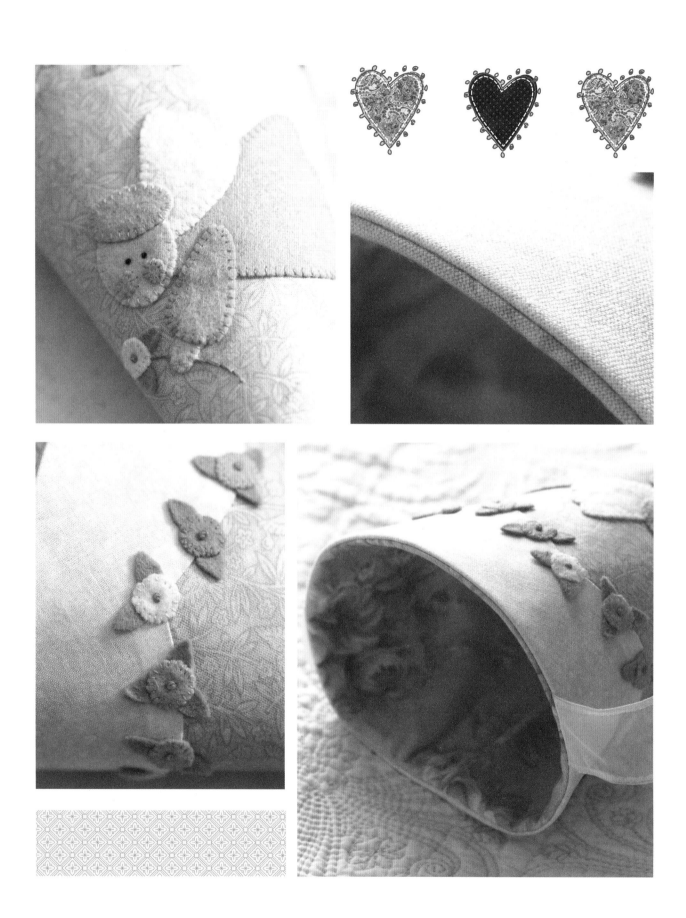

6 Stitch embroidery following Embroidery instructions, (below). Remove any tracing lines and allow to dry if necessary.

7 Right sides together, sew along the side seam (the straight edge). Trim at the bottom. Turn the right side out. Pin or tack (baste) the ribbon to the front, following the template, matching one end of each ribbon to the top edge of the cone. Remember your left over flower in step 5? Whipstitch this on now with it's leaves, covering the seam.

8 Use a ⅜in (1cm) seam for the lining for a better fit inside the cone. Right sides together, sew your lining piece along the same edge as before but leave a 3in–4in (7.5cm–10cm) opening for turning, approximately 2in (5cm) from the top edge. Clip at the bottom. Do not turn right side out.

9 Matching seams, put the front of the cone inside the lining piece, stuffing all the ribbon inside too. Match and pin edges. Sew all around the top edge through all

layers and ribbons. Trim the edge to ⅛in (3mm). Reach inside the opening in the lining and pull everything the right side out.

10 Whipstitch the opening closed. Tuck the lining into the cone and press along top edge. Fill with flowers or chocolates and tie a bow at the top to finish.

>> Embroidery

- French knot a centre for each flower with three strands of yellow **(1)**.
- Backstitch a stem on the angel's flower with three strands of green **(2)**.
- French knot eyes on the angel with two strands of black **(3)**.

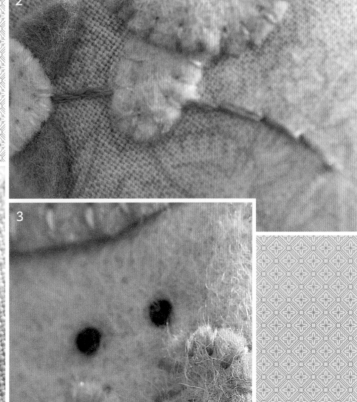

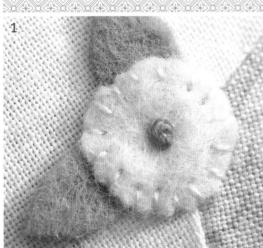

Hanging Pocket Quilt

Soft colours, sweet angels and a big heart to fill with lovely things, this hanging quilt is as pretty as a picture and will take you about a week. The pale green subtly complements the flowers but you can change the colour to your mother's favourite.

You will need...

- Light green fabric: 18in x 44in (46cm x 112cm)
- Off-white fabric: 18in x 44in (46cm x 112cm)
- Yellow fabric: 8in x 20in (20cm x 50cm)
- Pink fabric: 7in x 8in (18cm x 20cm)
- Pink wool felt: 12in x 12in (30cm x 30cm)
- Off-white and yellow wool felt: 8in x 8in (20cm x 20cm)
- Peach wool felt: 7in x 7in (18cm x 18cm)
- Green wool felt: 10in x 10in (25.5cm x 25.5cm)
- Freezer paper: 10in x 10in (25.5cm x 25.5cm)
- Double-sided fusible webbing: 11in x 11in (28cm x 28cm) .
- Backing fabric: 23in x 20in (58.5cm x 50cm)
- Lightweight wadding (batting): 20in (50cm) square and 8in x 10in (20cm x 25.5cm)
- Embroidery threads (floss)

Finished size:
21in x 18in (53.3cm x 46cm)

Templates for this project can be found on pages 110–111

» Directions

1 Cut an 11in x 11in (28cm x 28cm) centre square from the green fabric. Using the template, cut out the circle from off-white fabric and fuse to the centre square with double-sided fusible webbing. Or for a turned under appliqué circle, add ¼in (6mm) all around the template, turn under then glue or pin in place and whipstitch round.

2 To assemble the borders, cut four 2½in x 11in (6.5cm x 28cm) strips from green fabric and eight 1½in x 11in (4cm x 28cm) strips from off-white fabric. Sew the strips together so that each green strip is bordered by an off-white one on both 11in (28cm) sides. Now you have four strips 11in x 4½in (28cm x 11.5cm). Sew two of these to the sides of the green centre square and press seams open.

3 Cut four 4½in x 4½in (11.5cm x 11.5cm) blocks from green fabric. Sew one to each end of the remaining border strips and press seams open. Now sew these borders to the top and bottom of the quilt top and press seams again.

4 Using the templates, trace the wool felt appliqué pieces to freezer paper, iron on to the corresponding wool felt and cut out. Referring to the templates and photo (left), glue or pin in place, noting the points where felt pieces overlap, for example the leaves and the angel's dress, legs and wing.

5 Following the template, trace the embroidery lines for eyes and flower centres to the wool felt pieces. Trace the flower stem to the corner squares.

6 Back the quilt top with 20in x 20in (50cm x 50cm) lightweight wadding (batting) by pinning, tacking (basting) or with spray adhesive, to create a quilted effect while stitching.

7 Whipstitch the appliqué pieces using one strand of matching embroidery thread (floss). Leave the leaves free, holding in place with the whipstitch round the flowers.

8 Embroider following Embroidery instructions (page 65). Remove any tracing lines and allow to dry if necessary.

9 Cut out two large hearts ¼in (6mm) larger than the template out of yellow fabric. One is the front, one is the back. Cut one small heart ¼in (6mm) larger than the template from pink fabric. Turn under ¼in

(6mm) along the edge and whipstitch in place on top of one yellow heart. Back this heart piece with the 8in x 10in (20cm x 25.5cm) wadding (batting), trimming the wadding (batting) to fit. Appliqué the flowers as shown in the template, following steps 4 and 7 above. Embroider the flowers following Embroidery instructions (page 65).

10 Right sides together, sew the two yellow hearts together, leaving an opening for turning. Clip to points, trim and turn the right side out. Whipstitch the opening closed.

11 With three strands of embroidery thread (floss) and using a blanket stitch, sew the heart to the quilt front as shown on the template and photo (left) Leave an opening for the pocket as shown.

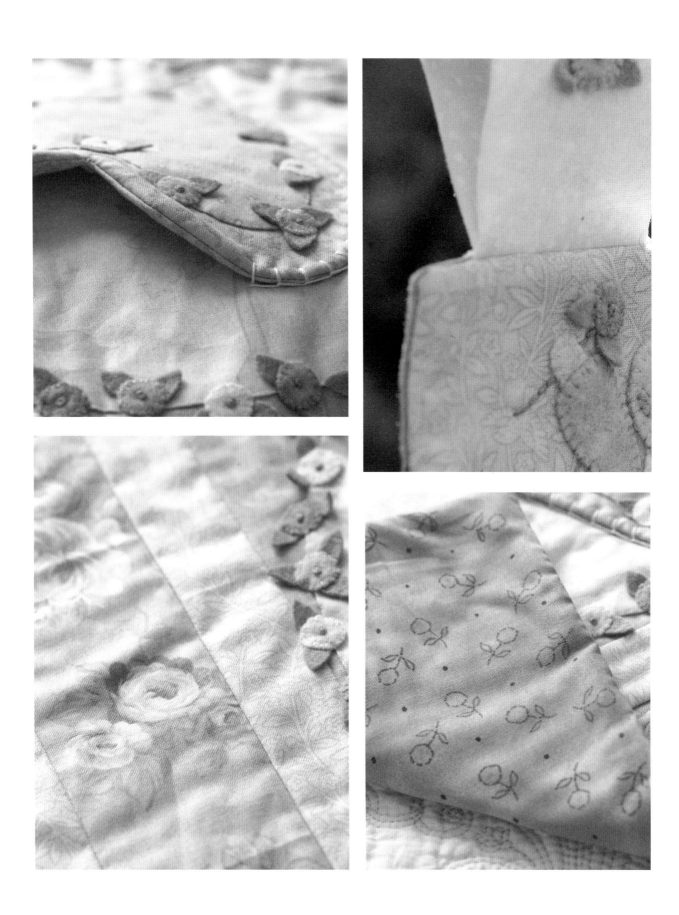

12 For the tabs, cut four 7in x 4½in (19cm x 11.5cm) rectangles from off-white fabric. Sew right sides together along the 7in (18cm) edge. Turn the right side out and press. Fold in half so each tab is 3½in x 2in (8.9cm x 5.1cm) and the seam runs down the middle inside. Mark the spot where the flower will go (approximately 1½in (4cm) from the folded edge). Sew a flower with three leaves following step 7 above (leaving the leaves free as before).

Pin or tack (baste) the tabs to the quilt top about 1½in (4cm) from each edge and 3in (7.5cm) apart, with the edges of the tabs and quilt lined up.

13 Right sides together, sew the backing fabric to the quilt top, catching the tabs in the seam and leaving an opening for turning. Clip the corners and trim. Turn through, whipstitch the opening closed and fill the pocket with dried or fabric flowers to finish.

> **» TIP**
>
> *Poles to hang up the quilt can be purchased from craft suppliers in many different styles and sizes. Make sure you choose one that will fit comfortable through the tabs, no more than 1½in (4cm) diameter.*

» Embroidery

- French knot a centre for each flower with three strands of yellow **(1)**.
- Backstitch a stem on the angel's flower with three strands of green **(2)**.
- French knot eyes on the angel with two strands of black **(3)**.

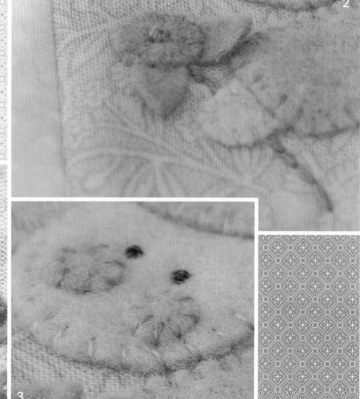

Hearts & Home

Moving into a new home is an exciting and hectic time for anyone. Why not bless your friend or loved one's new nest with a handmade present to mark the occasion? All of the house warming gifts are very quick and simple to create and can be made in fabric or wool felts.

Help your friends to settle in with a cushion made in fabrics to match the colours that they have decorated their new home. This lovely and thoughtful gift will be truly appreciated and leave them with a warm and glowing feeling.

The Greeting would be perfect hung on the front door of a friend's new abode to welcome visitors as they arrive and is sure to make everyone who comes to call feel right at home.

Present the Candle Mat with a pretty glass votive and a fragrant candle and you will have a sweet, simple gift that will bring light and warmth to any room.

Hearts & Home Greeting

This is the perfect gift to create for a last-minute invitation to a house warming party. The Hearts and home greeting, made just from wool felt, is a quick 2½ hour project so you may have just enough time to make the cute little Candle mat to go with it.

You will need...

- Tan wool felt: 5in x 9in (12.7cm x 22.7cm)
- Green wool felt: 6in x 10in (15.2cm x 25.4cm)
- Ecru wool felt: 3in x 2½in (7.6cm x 6.4cm)
- Red wool felt: 5in x 3in (12.7cm x 7.6cm)
- Brown wool felt: 2in x 3in (5.1cm x 7.6cm)
- Freezer paper: 12in x 12in (30.5cm x 30.5cm)
- Tan ribbon: 12in (30.5cm) of ¼in (6mm)
- Embroidery threads (floss)
- Glue

Finished size:
5in x 9in (12.7cm x 22.7cm)

Templates for this project can be found on page 117

›› Directions

1 Following the template on page 117, trace the background for the greeting on to freezer paper. Iron this to the tan wool felt and then cut out. Save the leftover pieces of tan felt for the windows.

2 Trace the hearts, chimney, door, roof, house and windows on to freezer paper from the templates. Iron these designs to the wool felt colours: hearts and chimney in red; door and roof in brown; house in ecru and windows in tan. Cut out two hearts, one house, one roof, one door, one chimney and five windows.

3 Using the template, trace the lines for the vines and leaves on to the tan background piece with a wash-away pen, or embroider them freehand. Trace or freehand embroider the little heart on to the house and the windowpanes on to the windows. Glue the felt pieces to the tan background following the template and photo (above).

4 Using one strand of matching thread (floss), whipstitch all the pieces in place.

5 To complete the embroidery follow the embroidery instructions below.

6 Remove any tracing lines with a damp sponge and allow to dry if necessary.

7 Pin or glue the ribbon to the tan background of the Greeting where shown on the template.

8 Pin or glue the completed appliquéd top to the green wool felt backing. Whipstitch in place, all around the edge, taking in the ribbon. Trim the backing ¼ in (6mm) away from the top edges. Your greeting is complete.

Using the same house and heart motifs as the Greeting and following the template on page 116, the quick and easy wool felt Candle Mat will take two to three hours and is a warming touch to any home. Given with a little scented candle, this is a sweet and simple token.

To give the background piece of the Greeting a charming vintage look I dyed the ecru felt with tea, then created the aged look of the felt by spotting the tan background with stronger tea.

>> Embroidery

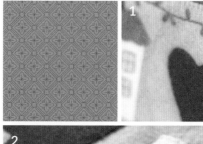

- Backstitch the vine around the background with three strands of green (1).
- Lazy daisy stitch leaves on the vine with three strands of green (1).
- Backstitch around each window with three strands of brown. Backstitch the windowpanes with one strand of brown (2).
- French knot the doorknob with three strands of dark brown (2).
- Backstitch a little red heart on the house with three strands of red (2).

Little Cushion

Create an heirloom quality to this special gift by using needle turn appliqué specially coordinated with the fabrics. The Little Cushion should take about one full day and so when you know the moving date plan ahead to create a truly personal token of good luck.

You will need...

- Tan fabric: 6in x 10in (15.2cm x 25.4cm)
- Green fabric: 6in x 10in (15.2cm x 25.4cm)
- Complementary green fabric: 6in x 10in (15.2cm x 25.4cm)
- Off-white fabric: 3in x 2½in (7.6cm x 6.4cm)
- Red fabric: 5in x 3in (12.7cm x 7.6cm)
- Brown fabric: 2in x 3in (5.1cm x 7.6cm)
- Glue or double-sided fusible webbing: 4in x 8in (10.2cm x 20.3cm)
- Stuffing: 8oz (250g)
- Lightweight wadding (batting): 6in x 11in (15.2cm x 27.9cm)
- Embroidery threads (floss)

Finished size:
5½in x 9½in (14cm x 24.1cm)
Templates for this project can be found on page 117

›› Directions

1 Following the template on page 117, trace the background shape on to the tan fabric. Add ¼in (6mm) all around if you choose to turn the edges. Alternatively, trace the background (without adding a seam allowance) on to double-sided fusible webbing and iron to the back of your tan fabric. Cut around the edge of this fused piece. Save leftover pieces of the tan fabric for the windows.

2 If you are using turned appliqué, add ¼in (6mm) to all appliqué pieces. Or, trace the hearts, house, door, roof, chimney, and windows on to the fusible webbing. Iron these designs on to the back of the fabrics shown in the photograph (above). Cut two hearts, one house, roof, door, chimney and five windows.

3 Using the template, trace the lines for the vines and leaves on to the tan background piece with a wash-away pen, or you can embroider them freehand. Trace or freehand embroider the little heart on to your house and windowpanes on to the windows.

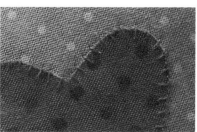

4 Glue the fabric house and heart pieces to the background following the photo (page 70) and the template for positioning. Appliqué the pieces by hand or, if you have used fusible webbing, iron them to the background.

5 Appliqué the tan background piece to the 6in x 10in (15.2cm x 25.4cm) piece of green backing fabric. You will use the piece of 6in x 10in (15.2cm x 25.4cm) complementary green fabric for the back of the cushion.

6 If you are using fusible appliqué, whipstitch all the pieces in place with one strand of matching enbroidery thread (floss).

7 Back the appliquéd front with the piece of lightweight wadding (batting) by pinning, tacking or with spray adhesive to create a quilted effect while stitching.

8 Use the instructions below to complete the embroidery. Remove any tracing lines with a damp sponge and allow to dry if necessary.

9 With right sides together, sew the back of the cushion to the appliquéd front leaving an opening for turning. Turn out and stuff. When you have finished stuffing the cushion, whipstitch the opening closed. Your gorgeous cushion is now complete!

›› Embroidery

- Backstitch the vine around the background with two strands of green (1).
- Lazy daisy stitch leaves on the vine with two strands of green (1).
- Backstitch around each window with two strands of brown. Backstitch the windowpanes with one strand of brown (2).
- Backstitch a little red heart on the house with two strands of red (2).
- French knot the doorknob with two strands of dark brown (3).

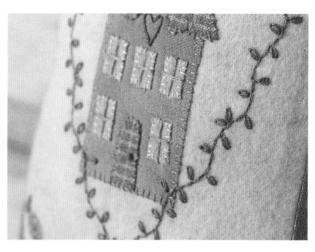

This little hanging cushion makes a quick variation project. Using the same house design and the pattern on page 118, you can change the colour palette of the appliqué to personalise the cushion, embroider the vine in a heart shape and add borders. Or for modest simplicity, leave out the appliqué and embroider the outlines on the house instead (below).

House Warming Quilt

Log cabin blocks create a classic quilt border to a cozy house, which is surrounded by a heart-shaped vine created by backstitch and lazy daisies. This is such a rewarding project, involving quite a bit of detail, so set aside a week to complete it.

You will need...

- Ecru fabric: 18in x 44in (45.7cm x 112cm)
- Print fabrics in green, blue, purple, ecru and red for borders: 4½in x 44in (11.4cm x 112cm)
- Green fabric for borders and binding: 11in x 44in (28cm x 112cm)
- Brown fabric for appliqué: 7in x 7in (17.8cm x 17.8cm)
- Light brown, blue, light blue, red and light green fabrics for appliqué: 6in x 6in (15.2cm x 15.2cm)
- Pink, rose, purple, and blue fabrics for flower appliqué: 5in x 5in (12.7cm x 12.7cm)
- Double-sided fusible webbing: 18in x 10in (45.7cm x 25.5cm)
- Lightweight wadding (batting): 25in x 25in (63.5cm x 63.5cm)
- Backing fabric: 25in x 25in (63.5cm x 63.5cm)
- Embroidery thread (floss)

Finished size:
23in x 23in (58.4cm x 58.4cm)

Templates for this project can be found on pages 124–125

›› Directions

1 Cut a 13½in x 13½in (34.3cm x 34.3cm) piece from the ecru fabric to form the centre of the quilt.

2 For the inner border, cut two 13½in x 1½in (34.3cm x 3.8cm) strips of green fabric, sew to the sides of the ecru square and press seams open. Cut two 15½in x 1½in (39.4cm x 3.8cm) strips of

green fabric, sew to the top and bottom of the ecru square and press seams open.

3 To make the blocks for the middle border, cut a 1½in x 1½in (3.8cm x 3.8cm) piece of ecru fabric for each block centre. Sew the borders on in the log cabin style, using four different print fabrics for the block sides (see the photo page 77). First cut a 1½in x 1½in (3.8cm x 3.8cm) piece of print fabric, sew to the side of the block centre and press the seam open. Next cut two 1½in x 2½in (3.8cm x 6.4cm) pieces from different print fabrics. Sew one to the side, press open and then sew the other to form the third side of the block centre. Press again. For the final side, cut a 1½in x 3½in (3.8cm x 8.9cm) piece of print fabric, sew to the last side of the block and press open. You need to make a total of twenty-four 3½in (8.9cm) blocks for the middle border.

4 Sew five of these 3½in (8.9cm) blocks together for each upright side of the centre border. Sew to the sides of the inner border and press seams open. Sew seven of these 3½in (8.9cm) blocks together to form the top and bottom of the centre border. Sew in place and press open.

5 For the outer ecru border, cut two 1½in x 21½in (3.8cm x 54.6cm) strips of ecru fabric, sew to the sides and press seams open. Cut two 1½in x 23½in (3.8cm x 59.7cm)

strips of ecru fabric, sew to the top and bottom and press seams open.

6 Trace all applique pieces on to double-sided fusible webbing. Following the template and photos, fuse on to the relevant fabrics. Cut out and fuse to the quilt top. With a single strand of matching embroidery thread (floss) whipstitch all the appliqué pieces to the quilt top.

7 Trace embroidery lines on to the centre block of the quilt top, the ecru centres of the border blocks and the outer border.

8 Back your quilt top with lightweight wadding (batting) by pinning, tacking (basting or with fabric adhesive, to create a quilted effect while stitching.

9 Stitch all the embroidery work following the embroidery directions below. Remove any tracing lines with a damp sponge and allow to dry if necessary.

10 Back the finished quilt top with backing fabric. Quilt as desired and bind to finish (see binding instructions page 105).

›› Embroidery

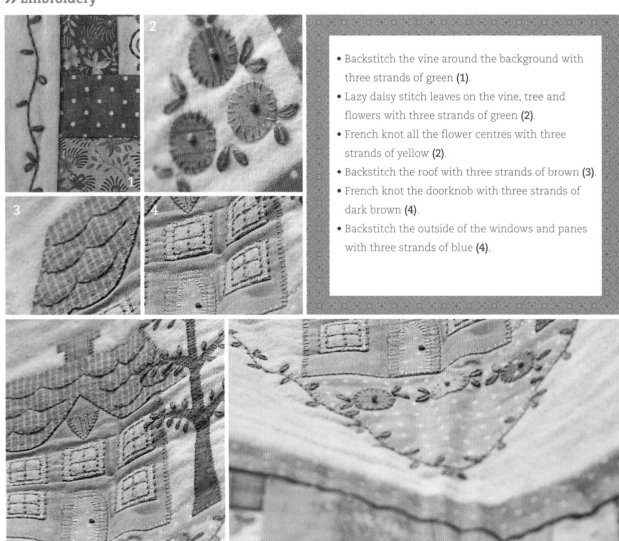

- Backstitch the vine around the background with three strands of green **(1)**.
- Lazy daisy stitch leaves on the vine, tree and flowers with three strands of green **(2)**.
- French knot all the flower centres with three strands of yellow **(2)**.
- Backstitch the roof with three strands of brown **(3)**.
- French knot the doorknob with three strands of dark brown **(4)**.
- Backstitch the outside of the windows and panes with three strands of blue **(4)**.

The same quilt but a different look, achieved by tracing the appliqué designs on to the centre block and embroidering along the lines. Limit the colours of the embroidery to emphasize the simplicity. Allow a week to finish.

Friendship

These gifts are for very special friends
– those kindred spirits who share your
love of sewing and crafting. The little Pin
cushion from felt and fabric with appliqué
flowers is so quick and easy to make
and yet will be brought into use day after
day. If you belong to a sewing group,
why not make one for each of your fellow
members to bind your friendship?

The Sewing kit holder is decorated with
hearts and delicate miniature flowers. Fill
with needles, thread, scissors and other
essentials, fold it up and your lucky friend
can pop it in a bag and enjoy her hobby
wherever she goes.

A gift for a special occasion, the
Friendship quilt is fun as well as
decorative. With sewing machine,
scissors, needle and thread lovingly
embroidered, it is something your friend
can treasure forever.

Pin Cushion

The classics are always the best. Practical and pretty, this soft pin cushion in time-honoured style will take just two to three hours but have lasting value.

You will need...

- Pink fabric: 7in x 14in (18cm x 35.5cm)
- Ecru wool felt: 4in x 4in (10cm x 10cm)
- Pink wool felt: 3in x 3in (7.5cm x 7.5cm)
- Freezer paper: 6in x 6in (15.5cm x 15.5cm)
- Lightweight wadding (batting): 7in x 14in (18cm x 35.5cm)
- Handful of stuffing
- Embroidery threads (floss)

Finished size:

5in circle x 1¾in tall (13cm x 4.5cm)

You will find the template for this project on page 112

›› Directions

1 Using the template, cut two circles from pink fabric.

2 Back both circles with very lightweight wadding (batting) by pinning, tacking (basting) or with spray adhesive.

3 Using the template and photo (above) trace and cut out the appliqué pieces and glue to the centre of one pink circle. Using one strand of matching embroidery thread (floss), whipstitch round the appliqué pieces.

4 Trace embroidery lines following the template. Stitch following Embroidery directions (right). Remove tracing lines and allow to dry if necessary.

5 Right sides together, sew the circles together, leaving an opening for turning. Turn through, stuff, then whipstitch the opening closed.

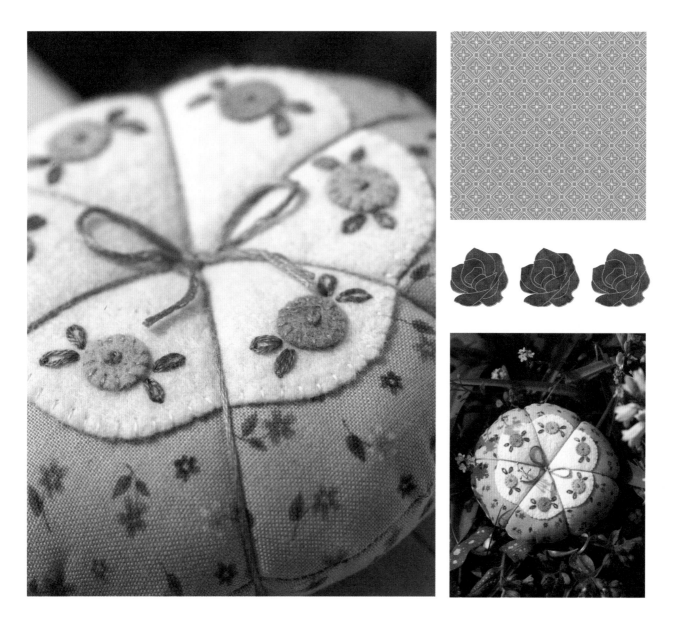

6 Take a long length (at least 36in/91.5cm) of six strand pink embroidery thread (floss) and a long needle. From the centre line marked on the template, loop the thread (floss) from top to bottom, up to the top centre again, then to the bottom into a hexagon, pulling tight each loop and centering. Knot off on the top. Tie a little bow in the middle with extra thread (floss) and glue to the top.

» Embroidery

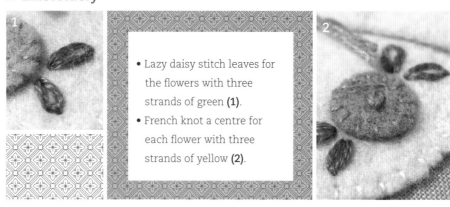

- Lazy daisy stitch leaves for the flowers with three strands of green **(1)**.
- French knot a centre for each flower with three strands of yellow **(2)**.

Sewing Kit Holder

Allow one to two days for the handiest of holders that folds up compactly and yet holds all the essential kit for sewing on the go.

You will need...

- Tan fabric: 9in x 16in (23cm x 40.5cm)
- Pink print fabric: 9in x 25in (23cm x 65.5cm)
- Fusible interfacing: 18in x 44in (46cm x 112cm)
- Ribbon: 20in x ¼in (50cm x 6mm)
- Ribbon: 108in x ⅛in (274.5cm x 3mm)
- Ecru wool felt: 12in x 12in (30cm x 30cm)
- Pink wool felt: 8in x 8in (20cm x 20cm)
- Freezer paper: 14in x 14in (35.5cm x 35.5cm)
- Small amount of stuffing
- Embroidery threads (floss)

Finished size: 7in x 22in (18cm x 56cm) open, 7in x 5in (18cm x 13cm) closed

Templates for this project can be found on pages 112–113

» Directions

1 Cut four 7½in x 6in (19cm x 15.5cm) pieces for the inside of the holder, two out of tan fabric and two out of pink.

2 Sew these four together along the 7½in (19cm) edge alternating tan, pink, tan, pink. The finished size should be 7½in x 22½in (19cm x 57cm).

3 Back this piece with 7in x 22in (18cm x 56cm) fusible interfacing to strengthen it. Centre and press to the wrong side.

4 Turn to the right side and, with a wash-away pen, mark where your topstitching will go, ¼in (6mm) from seams. Mark a ¼in (6mm) seam line along the top, bottom and sides.

5 Cut two front pieces from pink fabric 7½in x 11½in (19cm x 29.2cm). Cut 10in (25.5cm) of ¼in (6mm) ribbon and pin or tack (baste) one end at the midpoint on one of the pieces along the 7½in (19cm) edge. Sew this pink piece to the other piece, catching the ribbon in the seam. You should now have one piece 7½in x 22½in (19cm x 57cm). Back this with 7in x 22in (18cm x 56cm) fusible interfacing as you did for the inside (step 3).

6 Using the templates, trace all the appliqué pieces on to freezer paper. Press the freezer paper templates to the corresponding wool felts and cut out.

7 For the pin cushion heart, take one large heart in pink, one small heart in off-white and three pink flowers. Pin or glue these all together following the template and photo (below right) and whipstitch down with a single strand of stranded cotton (floss). Embroider flowers and leaves following Embroidery directions (page 85). Pin in place in the centre of the tan inside end piece, following the template. With two strands of matching embroidery thread (floss), whipstitch down leaving an opening. Place a small amount of stuffing inside and whipstitch to close.

8 For the scissors holder, take one large heart in off-white, one small heart in pink and three off-white flowers. Glue, whipstitch and embroider as above. With two strands of matching embroidery thread (floss), whipstitch in place where shown on the template, leaving an opening for scissors.

9 For the ruler pocket, cut one piece 6½in x 2½in (16.5cm x 6.5cm) from the tan fabric. Turn

under ¼ in (6mm) along the lengths. Cut a piece of interfacing to size and iron on the wrong side to add strength. Fold in half wrong sides together, so that your pocket is now 3¼ in x 2in (8.2cm x 5cm). On one side, add the flower appliqué, whipstitch down and embroider following Embroidery instructions (opposite). Pin or glue in place and topstitch ⅛in (3mm) from the sides leaving the top open for a ruler.

10   Appliqué and embroider all the little wool felt flowers to the inside corners, referring to the templates (pages 112–113) for positioning. Make sure they are within your seam lines.

11   Trace and cut out the heart and flower pieces for the front appliqué. Following the template, pin and whipstitch in place and embroider following Embroidery instructions (opposite).

12   For the thread (floss) and scissor ties on the inside of

the holder, cut the ⅛in (3mm) wide ribbon into 10in (25.5cm) lengths. Tack (baste) these in the middle (so that 5in is loose on each side) at all the placement markings shown on the templates. Topstitch, zig-zag, or hand sew these in place.

13 Pin all loose ribbons to the inside to keep them from getting caught in seams.

14 Right sides together, making sure your pin cushion heart and front cover heart are lined up, sew all around the front and inside pieces, leaving an opening for turning. Clip the corners and trim. Turn the right side out and press. Slipstitch the opening closed.

15 Topstitch along the seams, ¼in (6mm) from the edge, following the template. Fill with sewing supplies and your kit holder is complete.

›› Embroidery

- French knot a centre for each flower with three strands of yellow **(1)**.
- Lazy daisy stitch leaves on the stems and flowers with three strands of green **(1)**.
- Backstitch stems on the ruler pocket with three strands of green **(2)**.

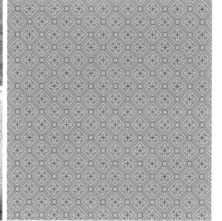

Friendship Quilt

Simple but stunning with only four blocks, a pieced border, a little appliqué and embroidery with a sewing theme, you can create this kindred quilt in four to seven days.

You will need...

- Pink fabric for borders: 27in x 44in (68.5cm x 112cm)

- Four off-white prints for borders, corners and block centres: 4½in x 44in (11.5cm x 112cm)

- Four brown fabrics for borders: 4½in x 44in (11.5cm x 112cm)

- Four green fabrics for border and binding: 4½in x 44in (11.5cm x 112cm)

- Four off-white fabrics for appliqué hearts: 5in x 5in (13cm x 13cm)

- Four pink fabrics for appliqué hearts and flowers: 5in x 5in (13cm x 13cm)

- Double-sided fusible webbing: 9in x 44in (23cm x 112cm)

- Lightweight wadding (batting): 24in x 24in (61cm x 61cm)

- Backing fabric: 24in x 24in (61cm x 61cm)

- Cutting mat and rotary cutter

- Embroidery threads (floss)

Finished size:
21in x 21in (53.3cm x 53.3cm)

Templates for this project can be found on pages 111–112

›› Directions

1 To make the four blocks, first cut four 4¼in x 4¼in (11cm x 11cm) centres from the off-white fabrics. From the brown fabric, cut eight 4¼in x 1in (11cm x 2.5cm) pieces. Sew to each side of the centres and press seams open. Cut eight 1in x 5¼in (2.5cm x 13.5cm) pieces, sew to each top and bottom of the centres and press seams open.

2 For the second, off-white, border, cut eight 5¼in x 1in (2.5cm x 13.5cm) pieces. Sew to each side of the blocks and press seams open. Cut eight 6¼in x 1in (16cm x 2.5cm) pieces. Sew to each top and bottom of the blocks and press seams open.

3 For the third, pink, border, cut eight 6¼in x 2¼in (16cm x 5.5cm) pieces. Sew to each side of the blocks and press open. Cut eight 9¾in x 2¼in (24.7cm x 5.5cm) pieces. Sew to each top and bottom of the blocks and press seams open.

4 Place your block on point (on the diagonal) on your cutting mat. With a rotary cutter, trim from the middle 4¼in (11cm) to each edge so that your block will be 8½in

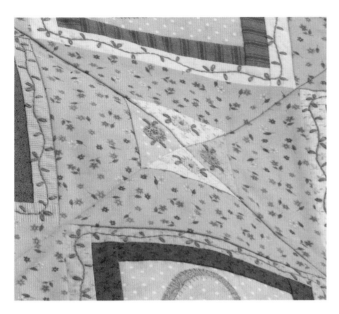

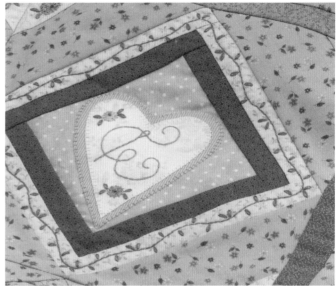

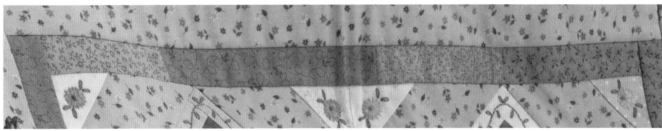

(21.5cm) from side to side and there are empty corners. There should be ¼in (6mm) from the point of the second, off-white border, too.

5 From your off-white fabric, cut eight 2¾in (7cm) squares. Cut in half once on the diagonal. Sew one triangle to each corner of each of your four patchwork pieces, referring to the template and photo (opposite). Press seams open. Trim so that each block is 8½in (21.5cm) square.

6 Sew the blocks together, two on top, two on the bottom.

7 From your different green fabrics, cut 1¼in (3.2cm) wide strips with lengths of 4in–7in

(10cm–18cm). Sew these together to create one continuous length. Cut this to make two 16½in x 1¼in (42cm x 3.2cm) strips for side borders and two 18in x 1¼in (46cm x 3.2cm) strips for the top and bottom borders. Sew the sides on first and press open seams and then the top and bottom, pressing again.

8 To add the last, pink, border cut two 18in x 2¼in (46cm x 5.5cm) strips. Sew to the sides and press seams open. Cut two 2¼in x 21½in (5.5cm x 54.5cm) strips, sew to the top and bottom and press seams open.

9 Using the templates, cut out four larger appliqué hearts from pink fabric and four smaller ones from off-white. Trace the embroidery designs on to the smaller hearts. Use double-sided fusible webbing to fuse the appliqué hearts to centres of each larger heart and then fuse these in position on the off-white centre blocks, as shown in the template and photo (opposite). Cut and fuse little pink flowers in different pink fabrics to the side triangles, central square and where shown on the hearts. Trace vines and leaves to the off-white border of each block.

10   Back the quilt top with wadding (batting) by pinning, tacking (basting) or with spray adhesive, to create a quilted effect while stitching.

11   Embroider following Friendship Embroidery directions (opposite). Remove any tracing lines and allow to dry if necessary.

12   Back the quilt and quilt as desired. Bind with green fabric (see Binding instructions page 105).

» TIP

The green border can be made from a single fabric or, for the 'scrappy' effect in my quilt, from several different fabrics joined together into lengths.

›› Embroidery

- Backstitch the sewing machine with two strands of black **(1)**.
- Backstitch the heart on the sewing machine with two strands of pink **(1)**.
- Backstitch the vines and stems with two strands of green **(2)**.
- Lazy daisy stitch leaves on vines, stems and flowers with two strands of green **(2)**.
- French knot a centre for each flower with three strands of yellow **(2)**.
- Backstitch the spool on the heart and sewing machine with two strands of tan **(2)**.
- Backstitch the needle and scissors with two strands of grey **(3)**.
- Backstitch all thread with two strands of yellow **(4)**.

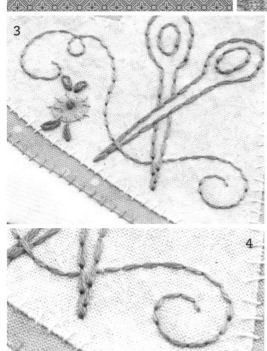

Christmas

Christmas is a wonderful, exciting holiday, where friends and relations celebrate together. It is a time for relaxing at home and enjoying the company of those close to you.

Make the receiving of gifts extra special by presenting them in a handmade gift bag. Fill these with all kinds of Christmas goodies and see your family's faces light up when they realise that they've got two presents in one.

Delightful tree decorations and a charming advent wallhanging are the perfect way to add that festive touch to your home. Choose special treats and gifts to slot into the beautifully decorated pockets of the wallhanging, and surprise your loved ones every day of advent. Adorable little angels, candy canes, snowmen and reindeer are just some of the enchanting motifs that give the wallhanging its festive charm. Have yourself a very merry Christmas!

Tree Decorations

When you receive a last minute festive party invitation, create one of these delightful tree decorations as a truly personal gift. You can make an ornament that your hostess will treasure in record time; each one should take 2½ hours.

You will need...

- White wool felt: 4½in x 4½in (11.4cm x 11.4cm)
- Wool felt in a colour of your choice: 5in x 5in (12.7cm x 12.7cm)
- Ecru flannel: 4in x 4in (10.2cm x 10.2cm)
- Ribbon: 6in x ¼in (15.2cm x 6mm)
- Freezer paper: 6in x 6in (15.2cm x 15.2cm) per ornament
- Pieces of wool felt in red, green, yellow, blue, brown, and peach (for all ornaments): 4in x 4in (10.2cm x 10.2cm)
- Embroidery threads (floss)
- Glue or double-sided fusible webbing: 6in x 6in (15.2cm x 15.2cm)

Finished size of each: 4in (10.2cm) diameter circle

Templates for this project can be found on page 116

›› Directions

1 After deciding the number of decorations that you want to make, trace the scalloped background for each ornament on to freezer paper following the template on page 116. Iron the freezer paper on to white wool felt and cut out.

2 For the ecru centre of each decoration, trace the circle shapes on to double-sided fusible webbing, iron to the back of ecru fabric and cut out, following the traced line. For turned under appliqué, cut out the ecru fabric ¼ in (6mm) larger than the template.

3 Choose your ornament design. Trace the appliqué piece(s) from the templates on to freezer paper and iron to the corresponding wool felt colours, and cut out.

4 Trace from the template with a wash-away pen, or stitch the vine and leaves embroidery freehand. Stitch all the other embroidery work following the embroidery instructions for the Advent Wallhanging on page 102.

5 Glue the wool felt appliqué pieces in place on the centre circle of ecru fabric, following the photos (below). Now appliqué these fabric pieces to the white wool felt scalloped pieces (if you used fusible webbing, this isn't necessary).

6 Whipstitch the wool felt appliqué pieces using one strand of matching embroidery thread (floss).

7 Remove any tracing lines with a damp sponge and allow to dry if necessary.

8 Fold a 6in (15.2cm) long piece of ribbon in half and pin or glue to the top and back of the white scalloped piece. Glue the white scalloped top to the desired wool felt backing colour. With a matching strand of embroidery thread (floss), whipstitch the background to backing. Trim the backing ¼ in (6mm) away from the edge. Your Tree decorations are finished!

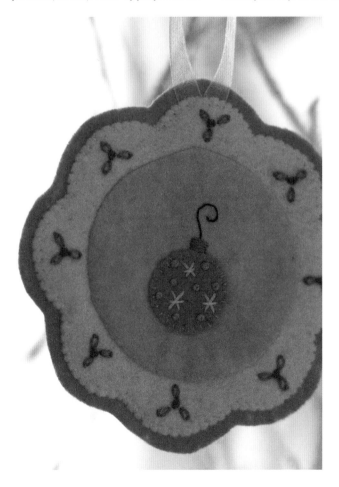 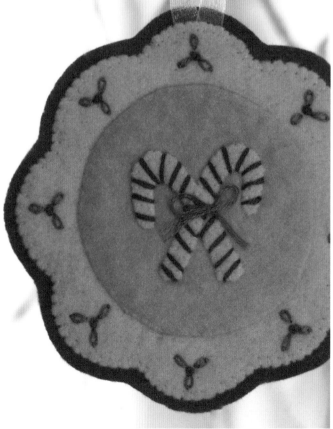

 **1 day project**

Christmas Gift Bag

With ribbons, buttons, piecing and appliqué you can have great fun spending a day creating this cheerful bag. The instructions here are for the bauble bag but you can easily change the size and appliqué motif following the photos and templates.

You will need...

- Ecru fabric: 25in x 9in (60.5cm x 22.9cm)
- Twenty-eight blocks, fourteen in green and fourteen in yellow: 1¼in x 1¼in (3.2cm x 3.2cm)
- Lining fabric: two pieces 7¼in x 8¾in (18.4xm x 22.2cm)
- Medium-weight fusible interfacing: two pieces 6¾in x 8¼in (17.1cm x 21cm)
- Red, yellow and green wool felts: 4in x 4in (10.2cm x 10.2cm)
- Four ½in (1.3cm) buttons
- Ribbon: four 12in (30.5cm) lengths
- Embroidery thread (floss)

Finished size:
7in x 8½in (17.8cm x 21.6cm)

Templates for this project can be found on page 119

›› Directions

1 Cut a 5¾in x 4¼in (14.6cm x 10.8cm) piece of ecru fabric for the centre of the bag.

2 For the inner border, take the twenty-eight 1¼in x 1¼in (3.2cm x 3.2cm) blocks and sew four sets of seven blocks together (one for each side) in an alternating pattern. Sew one set of blocks to each of the four sides of the bag centre, pressing seams open as you go along.

3 Cut four 7¼in x 1¼in (18.4cm x 3.2cm) strips of ecru fabric for the outer border. Sew each side of the outer border to the inner

border, pressing seams as you go.

4 To add stability to the bag, centre one of your pieces of fusible interfacing on the reverse of the assembled bag front, ¼ in (6mm) from the selvage edge.

5 Cut out the appliqué pieces from corresponding wool felts and glue or pin in place following the templates and photo (above). Using one strand of matching stranded cotton (floss), whipstitch the wool felt appliqué pieces in place.

6 Stitch the embroidery work following the Embroidery instructions on page 97.

7 Cut a piece of ecru fabric 7¼ in x 8¾ in (18.4cm x 22.2cm) for the back of your bag. Take your second piece of fusible interfacing and add to the piece of fabric for the bag back, as in step 4.

8 With right sides of the back and front of the bag facing, sew the two pieces together along the sides and bottom only. Trim the edges and clip the corners then turn right sides out and press.

9 Take your two pieces of lining fabric. Right sides together,

sew the sides and bottom together, leaving an opening for turning about 3in (7.6cm) along the bottom Trim the sides and clip the corners. Do not turn the right way out.

10 Put your front into your lining so that right sides are together and side seams are matching. Sew the front and lining together ¼in (6mm) from the top edge. Trim this ⅛in (3mm) from the edge. Reach into the opening in the lining and pull it right side out. Press the lining away from the bag front and then whipstitch or topstitch the opening closed. Tuck the lining into the bag and press along the top.

11 Choose ribbons in complementary colours for the handle. I chose to have handles on the front and back. See the Handles box on page 14 for more details on how to make different types of handle with ribbons.

Why not make a collection of bags to give your friends? See the templates on pages 119 for the heart, star and Santa bags.

» Embroidery

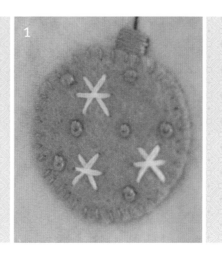

- Backstitch the vines with two strands of green.
- Lazy daisy stitch the leaves with two strands of green.
- French knot the berries with three strands of red.
- Backstitch the stars with two strands of white **(1)**.
- French knot the dots with three strands of either blue, green or red, a different colour for each bauble **(1)**.
- Backstitch the top of the bauble with three strands of grey **(1)**.
- Backstitch the hanger with one strand of black.

 1 week project

Advent Pocket Wallhanging

Every family member will know it is Christmas time when the advent pocket wallhanging is hung. This timeless keepsake will last for years but should take only a week to complete. Allow three or four days for the pockets and three more days for assembly of the back and borders.

You will need...

- Ecru flannel for pockets and borders: 36in x 44in x 36in (91.4cm x 111.8cm)
- Light green fabric for borders: 12in x 44in (30.5cm x 111.8cm)
- Red fabric for borders and tabs: 12in x 44in (30.5cm x 111.8cm)
- Backing fabric: 23in x 24in (58.4cm x 61cm)
- White wool felt: 15in x 15in (38.1cm x 38.1cm)
- Wool felt in red, green, yellow, blue, brown, and peach: 10in x 10in (25.4cm x 25.4cm)
- Freezer paper: 16in x 16in (40.6cm x 40.6cm)
- Medium-weight fusible interfacing: 36in x 18in (91.4cm x 45.7cm)
- Lightweight wadding (batting): 24in x 23in (61cm x 58.4cm)
- Embroidery thread (floss)
- Glue or 6in x 6in (15.2cm x 15.2cm) double-sided fusible webbing

Finished size:

25in x 21in (63.5cm x 53.3cm)

Templates for this project can be found on pages 116 and 119

>> Directions

1 Cut out twenty-five 5in x 3½in (12.7cm x 8.9cm) pieces of ecru fabric for the pocket fronts. Fold each pocket in half wrong sides together so that each front is 2½in x 3½in (6.4cm x 8.9cm). Attach a 2¼in x 3in (5.7cm x 7.6cm) piece of fusible interfacing to one side of this folded piece to add strength. This is the side you appliqué.

2 Following the template on page 116, trace the scalloped piece on to freezer paper and then iron to the white wool felt. Cut out twenty-five scalloped pieces. Again, following the templates, trace the festive designs on to freezer paper, iron to the corresponding wool felt colours, see photograph (above) and cut out. There are

three snowmen, three hearts, three stars, three candles, two trees, two baubles, two reindeer, two candy canes, two angels, two stockings, and one Santa Claus.

3 Trace from the template or embroider the designs freehand on to the scalloped pieces and festive designs following the Embroidery directions on page 102. Glue the wool felt appliqué pieces in place on the pocket fronts.

Be careful not to let your designs go past the ¼in (6mm) seam allowance along the bottom edge. The scalloped top should be level with the fold in the fabric, and the designs need to be in the middle of each pocket.

4 Whipstitch the wool felt appliqué pieces to the pocket fronts using one strand of matching embroidery thread (floss). Be careful not to catch the back of the fold in the stitching. This is meant to fold over and line the backs of the pockets to cover the knots and threads.

5 Cut out twenty-five pocket backs out of ecru fabric 3½in x 3½in (8.9cm x 8.9cm). Pin or baste the pocket front (back folded down) to each back with the bottom and side edges even. 1in (2.5cm) should be left on top for more embroidery work.

6 Cut twenty 3½in x 1in (8.9cm x 2.5cm) pieces of the light green fabric for the vertical pocket side borders. Sew one of

these pieces through all the layers to the right side of the first four pockets in each row. The fifth pocket in each row will have a joining border later.

Now join these pockets together into rows by sewing the left side of pockets 2–5 to the right side of pockets 1–4 in each row. Follow the photo (page 99) to check the order of the pocket designs. Press the seams towards the light green border.

7 Cut four 1½in x 17in (3.8cm x 43.2cm) strips of the light

green fabric for the horizontal borders. Join the rows together leaving the first row free of a top horizontal strip and the fifth row free of a bottom horizontal strip. Press the seams towards the light green borders. There will be a slight dimple in the joining points of the green borders, which I think adds character to the wallhanging.

8 Cut two 19½in x 1in (49.5cm x 2.5cm) strips of the light green fabric for the side borders.

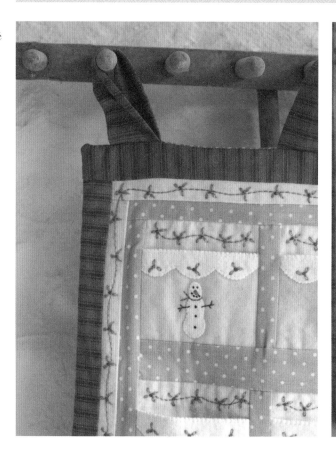

Sew to the sides, and press seams open. Cut two 1in x 18½in (2.5cm x 47cm) strips from the same fabric and sew to the top and bottom of the wallhanging. Press seams open.

9 Cut two 20½in x 1in (52.1cm x 2.5cm) strips of the ecru flannel. Sew to the sides of the wallhanging and press seams open. Cut two 1in x 19½in (2.5cm x 49.5cm) strips of the same fabric. Sew to the top and bottom and press the seams.

10 Cut two 21½in x 1½in (54.6cm x 3.8cm) strips of the red fabric for the final border. Sew to the sides and press seams open. Cut two 1½in x 21½in (3.8cm x 54.6cm) strips of the same fabric. Sew to the top and bottom of the wallhanging and press open.

11 Using a wash-away pen trace embroidery lines to the remaining 1in (2.5cm) top of each pocket and the ecru border, following the template on page 116.

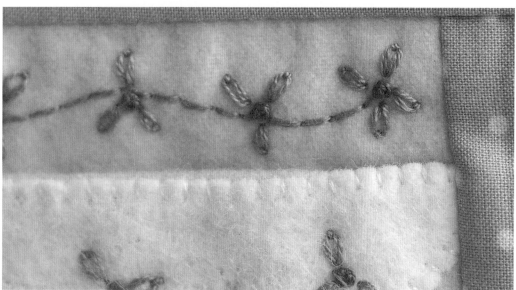

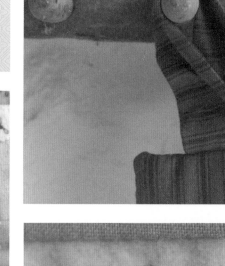

12 Attach lightweight wadding (batting) to the back the wallhanging by pinning, tacking (basting) or with fabric adhesive to create a 'quilted' effect while stitching. Stitch embroidery work following Embroidery instructions (right).

13 Remove any tracing lines with a damp sponge and allow to dry if necessary

14 Cut five 6in x 3½in (15.2cm x 8.9cm) strips of the red fabric. These will become the tabs on the top of the wallhanging. Fold each one in half along the 6in (15.2cm) edge, right sides together. Sew this edge. Turn the tabs right side out and press.

Fold in half to create a loop. Pin or tack (baste) the tabs along the top edge of the completed top, ensuring that the raw edges of the tabs are level with the edge of the wallhanging top and that spacing is equal between each tab.

15 With the right sides together, sew the 23in x 24in (58.4cm x 61cm) piece of backing fabric to the front, leaving an opening for turning. Clip the corners to minimize bulk and trim edges to ¼ in (6mm). Turn the wallhanging right side out and whipstitch the opening closed to finish the project. Hang and fill with goodies.

›› Embroidery

- Backstitch the vines with two strands of green.
- Lazy daisy stitch the holly leaves with two strands of green.
- French knot the berries with three strands of red.
- Snowman: backstitch the nose with two strands of orange. French knot eyes, mouth and buttons with one strand of black. Backstitch the arms with two strands of brown. Backstitch the scarf with two strands of blue **(1)**.
- Heart: French knot dots all round with three strands of pink **(2)**.
- Star: French knot a berry in the centre with three strands of red. Lazy daisy stitch the leaves with two strands of green. French knot dots at the points with three strands of yellow **(3)**.
- Tree: backstitch the garland with three strands of yellow. French knot the dot on the top of the tree with three strands of yellow. French knot the tree ornaments with three strands of blue **(4)**.
- Candles: French knot the berries with three strands of red. Lazy daisy stitch the leaves with two strands of green. Backstitch the flame highlights with two strands of orange. Backstitch the candlewicks with one strand of black **(5)**.
- Bauble: backstitch the stars with two strands of white. French knot the dots with three strands of yellow. Backstitch the top of the bauble with three strands of grey. Backstitch the hanger with one strand of black **(6)**.
- Reindeer: backstitch the antlers and legs with two strands of brown. Lazy daisy stitch the ears and tail with two strands of brown. French knot the nose with two strands of brown. Backstitch the collar with two strands of red. French knot the bells on the collar with two strands of yellow. French knot the eyes with one strand of black **(7)**.
- Candy canes: backstitch the stripes with three strands of red. Tie a bow around the centre and secure with glue **(8)**.
- Angel: backstitch the halo with three strands of yellow. French knot the dots on the dress with three strands of yellow. Backstitch the arms and legs with three strands of peach **(9)**.
- Stocking: French knot the dots with three strands of red.
- Santa Claus: lazy daisy stitch the moustache with three strands of white. French knot the eyes with one strand of black.

General Instructions

Using this book

- All seams are sewn with a ¼ in (6mm) seam allowance. Cutting instructions include a ¼ in (6mm) seam allowance.
- Appliqué design pieces are finished sizes. The appliqué templates on pages 108–125 do not include a ¼ in (6mm) allowance for turning under. If you choose to turn under your appliqué designs, add ¼ in (6mm) around the edges.
- The thicker lines in the templates are appliqué, the thinner lines are embroidery.

Tracing templates and designs

Trace designs by centering designs over a light source. This may be a light box or even a sunny window. Place your paper design to be traced first, then your fabric piece over this. It helps to tape your design so you may take a rest and come back to it if needed.

You can also trace the templates to freezer paper and iron the paper to fabric before cutting out (see Using wool felt, page 106). While more time consuming, it is precise. You may use the freezer paper again and again.

Use your favourite tracing tool to trace on to fabric. Mine is a blue wash-away pen. You may choose tailor's chalk, pencil or pen.

Backing with wadding (batting)

I like to make my quilt tops and have them traced and ready for the embroidery work. Then I back my tops with a lightweight quilt wadding (batting) to create a 'quilted' effect while stitching. You can hold the backing in place by pinning, tacking or with fabric spray adhesive, whichever you prefer.

This method gives you stability while stitching, allows the threads to carry over from point to point without the thread (floss) being seen from the front and, most importantly, plumps up the stitches so that they have body and are not flat.

Embroidery threads (floss)

For all the projects in this book I have used stranded cotton embroidery threads (floss), which are widely available in a vast array of colours. In the embroidery sections of each project, I have indicated colours to use, but you can, of course, change these as you like.

Embroidery threads (floss) are usually formed from six strands and can be split into single strands. The number of strands to use for each piece of work (one, two or three) is indicated in the instructions for each project.

Double-sided fusible webbing

Often sold as Bondaweb or Wonderweb, this can be used as a quick, alternative method of attaching an appliqué piece to a background fabric. One side looks like paper and you can trace the shape you want on to it (note that the shape will come out in reverse). Cut around roughly and iron on to the back of the felt or fabric you want to appliqué. Cut carefully on traced lines, peel off the paper backing and iron on to the background fabric to fuse.

If you are using this method for wool felt appliqué, you can leave the whipstitch edging out and move straight to embroidery.

Binding a quilt or cushion

- Trim backing and wadding so that the edges line up evenly with the top of the quilt or cushion.
- Cut lengths of binding fabric to a width of 2½in (6.5cm. You may need to join strips together to make sure there is enough to go all round plus a few inches extra for the corners and ends.
- Fold the left hand edge of the strip up to form a diagonal edge and press the binding strip in half across wrong sides together along the whole length (A).
- Place the binding strip against the raw edge of the right side of the quilt, an inch or two away from the corner and pin in place. Leaving the first inch (the tail) free, sew a ¼in (6mm) seam all the way along, stopping ¼in (6mm) from the next corner (B).

- Fold the binding up from the corner so you have a 45-degree angle, keeping the raw edges aligned, as shown in the diagram (C).
- Fold the binding back down again to line up with the right-hand edge of the quilt (D). Reverse stitch over the edge and continue sewing to within ¼in (6mm) of the next corner, then turn as you did before. When you reach the starting point, tuck the end into the folded tail and stitch over.
- Fold over the binding to the back of the quilt and stitch in place, folding the binding at each corner to form a neat mitre as shown in the diagram (E).

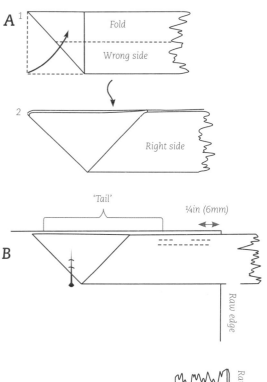

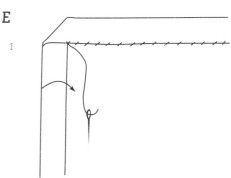

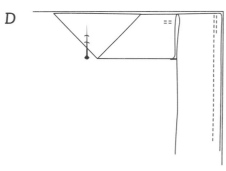

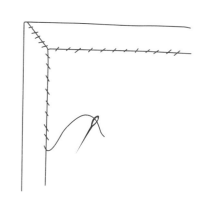

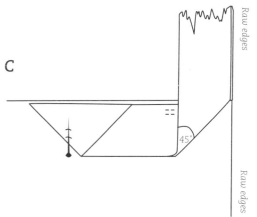

Using wool felt

Always pre-rinse your wool felts prior to use. Do this by running under warm water in the sink, rinsing until the water runs almost clear. Then, squeeze out excess water and allow to air dry before ironing. This makes sure all the dyes are out and the wool is shrunk to size. It is good to get into the habit of rinsing felt as soon as you buy it. Store it by colour and it will be ready to use whenever you need it.

Use freezer paper to cut your wool felt design pieces. Trace the appliqué design to the dull side of the freezer paper (there are no seams to turn under with wool-felt appliqué). With a dry iron, iron the shiny side of the paper on to the wool felt and it will stick temporarily. Cut out on traced lines and peel the paper from the wool felt. You may use the same freezer paper template many times.

Glue your wool felt appliqué pieces to your project. They only need the tiniest spots of glue to hold. This is a method I use with all appliqué. If you haven't done this in the past, you will love the fact that there are no pins to lose or catch threads. After gluing, I press all my pieces briefly with the iron. This anchors them and also makes the surface a little flatter and neater to whipstitch. Using one strand of embroidery thread (floss) matching the colour of the wool felt, I use a simple whipstitch to sew to the background for a very neat and finished look.

I use my favourite blue wash-away pen to mark embroidery lines to the wool felt. After stitching, I remove these lines with a very damp sponge, blotting the lines sparingly. Chalk also works well with wool felt. Using chalk you may simply brush the lines away. Wool felt does not trace very well so I hope you may get confident enough to apply the simple embroidery lines freehand. You will get very good at doing French knot dots and lazy daisy leaves on your own!

Stitches

WHIPSTITCH

This stitch is used to anchor appliqué to backing fabric. Bring the needle up ⅛in (3mm) into the appliqué. Move the needle horizontally ⅛in (3mm) and down into the backing fabric. On the wrong side, move the needle diagonally and forward ⅛in (3mm) up again into the appliqué piece and again ⅛in (3mm) down into the backing fabric. Repeat all around.

TOPSTITCH

This is done with your sewing machine. Using a ⅛in (3mm) to ¼in (6mm) straight stitch, sew through all layers, anchoring your pieces to the backing fabric.

SATIN STITCH

Bring the needle up to the top of the shape to fill in. Bring the needle back down horizontally across from the shape to the bottom. The next stitch is brought up right next to first stitch, then brought down right next to the previous second stitch. Fill in with stitches right next to each other until the entire space is filled.

LAZY DAISY

Bring the needle up to the top at the base of the stitch point (think of a teardrop – the base is the point, the round part is the loop). Bring the needle back down to base in the same hole without pulling the thread (floss) all the way through. Let the thread (floss) make a loop and bring the needle back up to the top of the loop at the required distance from the base. Catch the loop with your needle and pull until the thread (floss) loop is the shape of a teardrop. Then bridge the loop with a small stitch to anchor in place.

FRENCH KNOT

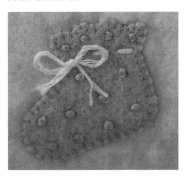

Bring the needle up to the top. Wrap the thread (floss) around the needle one, two or three times depending on the desired size of the knot (one loop small knot, two loops medium knot, three loops larger knot). Drop the needle back into the original hole, being careful not to let the loops unwrap. Pull the needle from the back, slowly drawing the thread (floss) through all the loops, creating a knot on the top.

RUNNING STITCH

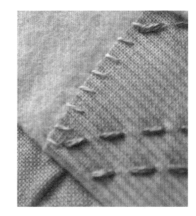

Bring the needle up to the top. Make a stitch at the required distance (usually ⅛in/3mm) bringing the needle down. Bring the needle back up, again leaving a distance in between. Repeat until complete.

SLIPSTITCH

This stitch is used to close openings. Bring the needle to the front of one side a scant ¹⁄₁₆in (1.5mm). Catch the other side with a scant ¹⁄₁₆in (1.5mm) stitch. Draw up the thread bringing these two sides together. Bring the needle back to the original side and repeat, moving across the opening until it is closed.

BACKSTITCH

Bring the needle up to the top. Moving backwards, bring the needle down ⅛in (3mm) from the original hole. Bring needle back up ⅛in (3mm) ahead of the original hole. Bring the needle back down into the original hole. Repeat, bringing the needle back up ahead of the last hole.

Templates

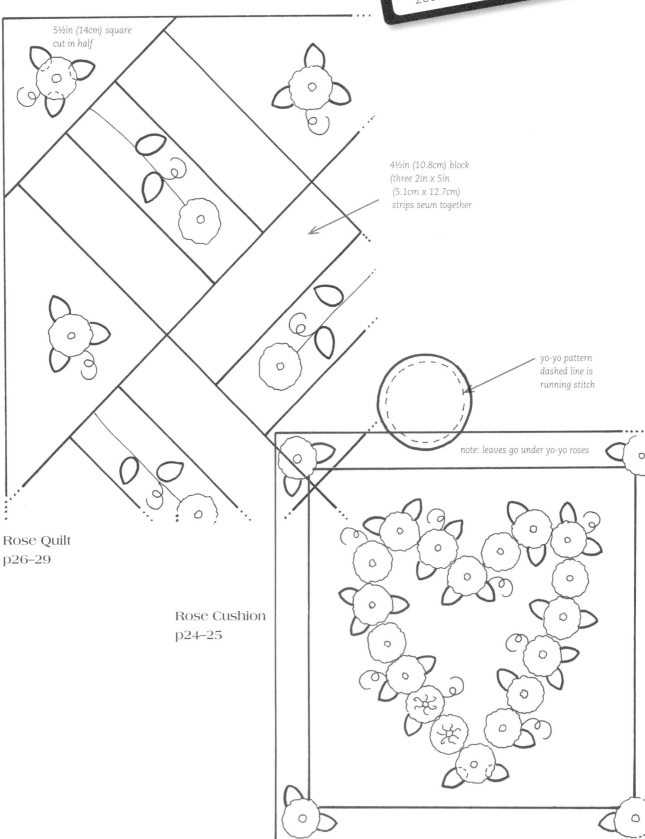

5½in (14cm) square cut in half

4½in (10.8cm) block (three 2in x 5in (5.1cm x 12.7cm) strips sewn together

yo-yo pattern dashed line is running stitch

note: leaves go under yo-yo roses

Rose Quilt
p26–29

Rose Cushion
p24–25

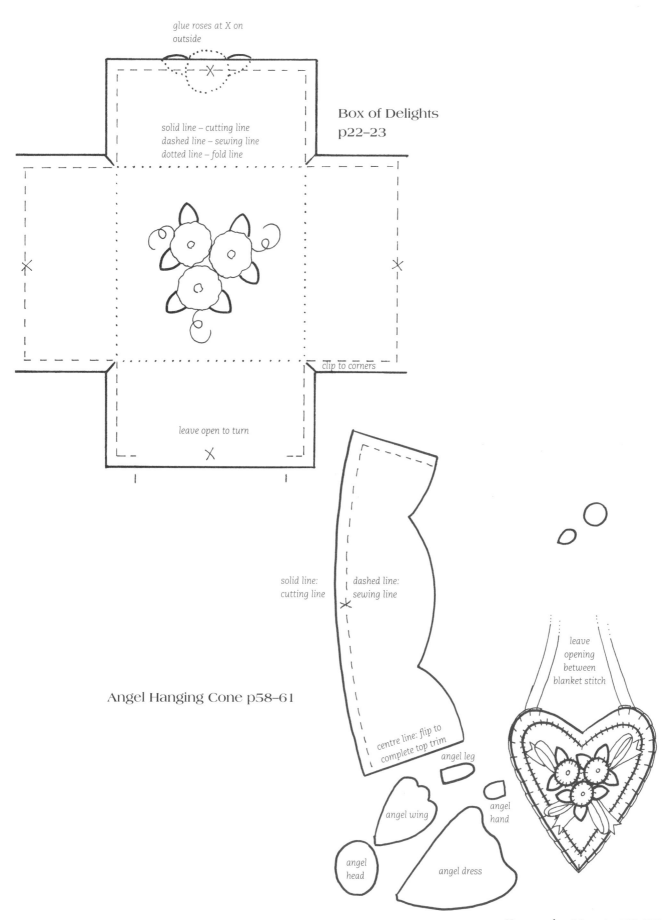

glue roses at X on outside

Box of Delights
p22–23

solid line – cutting line
dashed line – sewing line
dotted line – fold line

clip to corners

leave open to turn

Angel Hanging Cone p58–61

solid line:
cutting line

dashed line:
sewing line

centre line: flip to
complete top trim

angel leg

angel wing

angel hand

angel head

angel dress

leave
opening
between
blanket stitch

Keepsake Heart p56–57

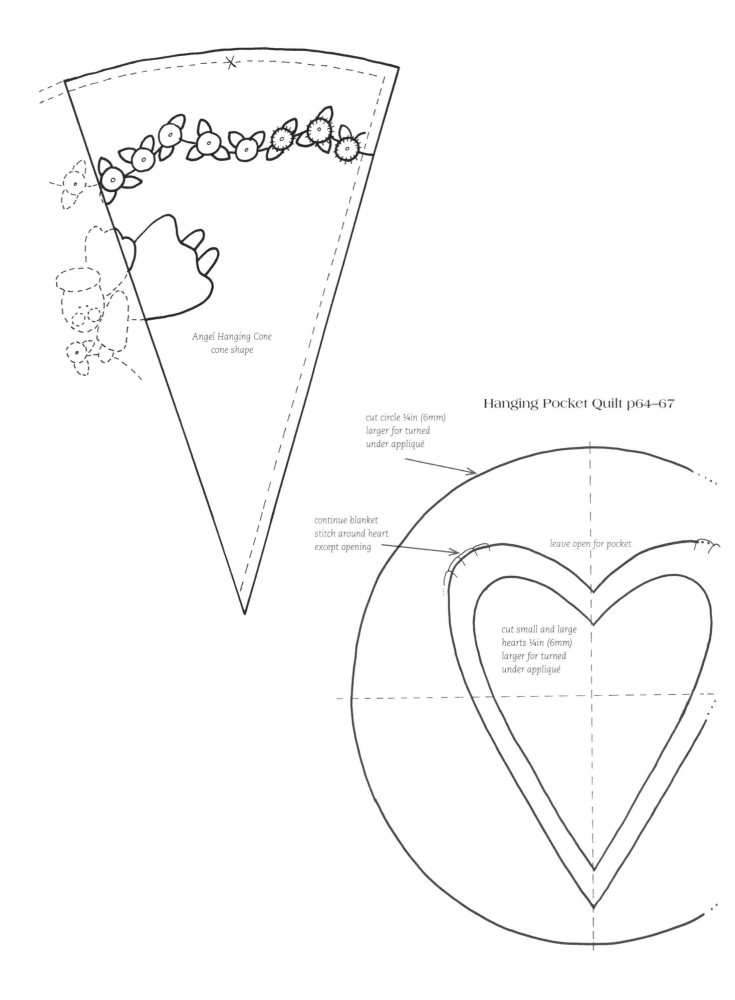

Angel Hanging Cone
cone shape

Hanging Pocket Quilt p64–67

cut circle ¼in (6mm)
larger for turned
under appliqué

continue blanket
stitch around heart
except opening

leave open for pocket

cut small and large
hearts ¼in (6mm)
larger for turned
under appliqué

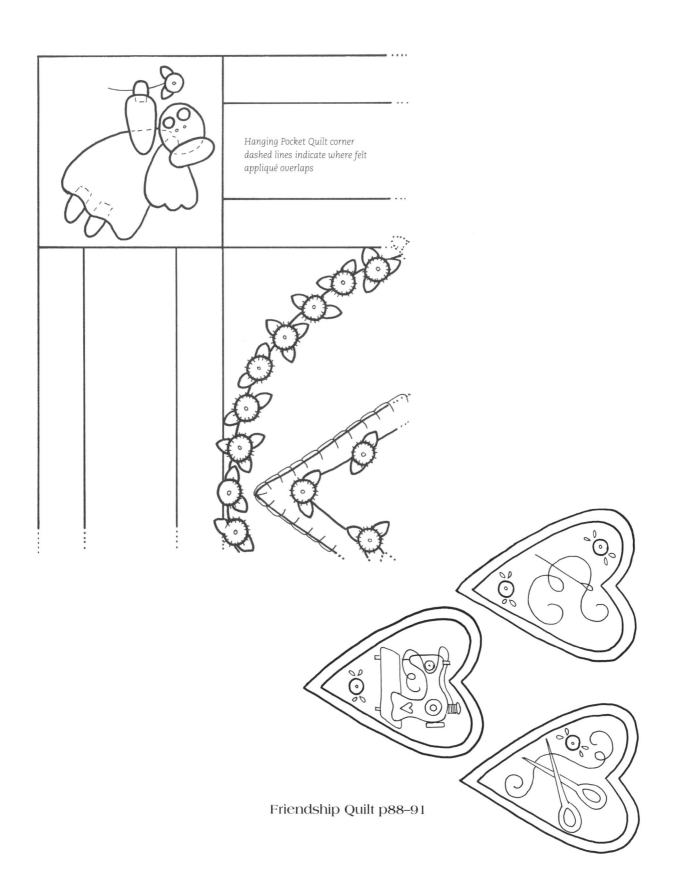

*Hanging Pocket Quilt corner
dashed lines indicate where felt
appliqué overlaps*

Friendship Quilt p88–91

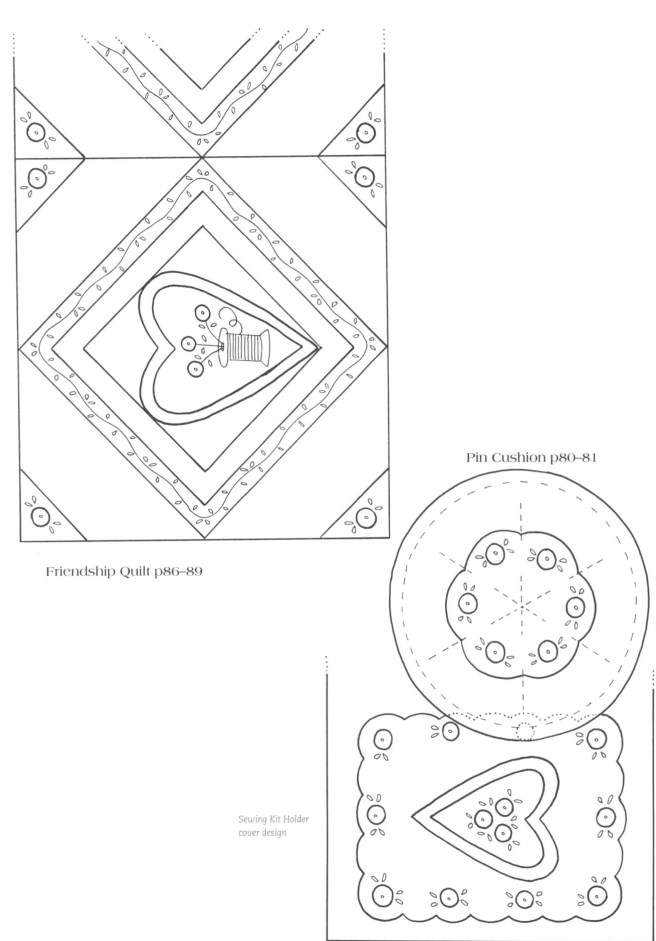

Friendship Quilt p86–89

Pin Cushion p80–81

*Sewing Kit Holder
cover design*

Sewing Kit Holder p82–85

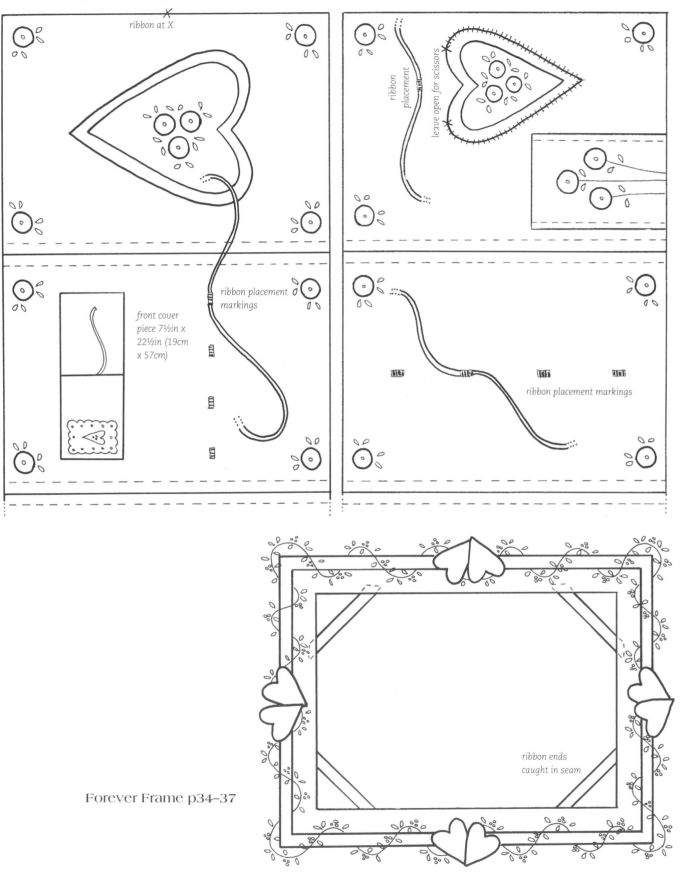

ribbon at X

ribbon placement

leave open for scissors

ribbon placement markings

front cover piece 7½in x 22½in (19cm x 57cm)

ribbon placement markings

ribbon ends caught in seam

Forever Frame p34–37

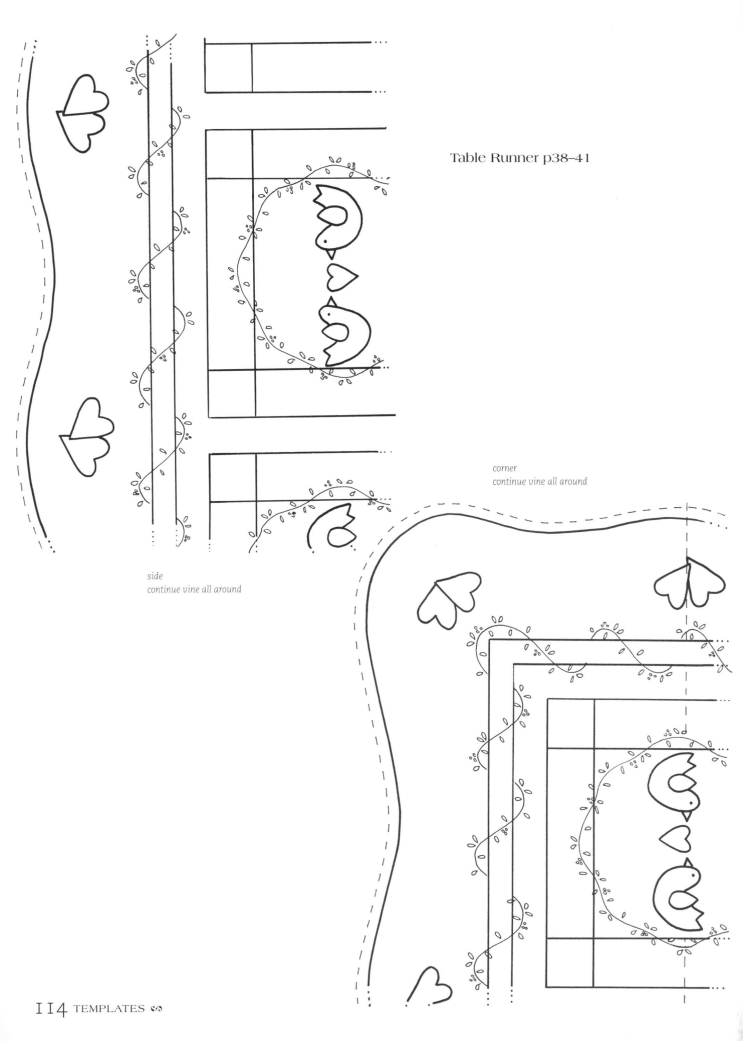

Table Runner p38–41

corner
continue vine all around

side
continue vine all around

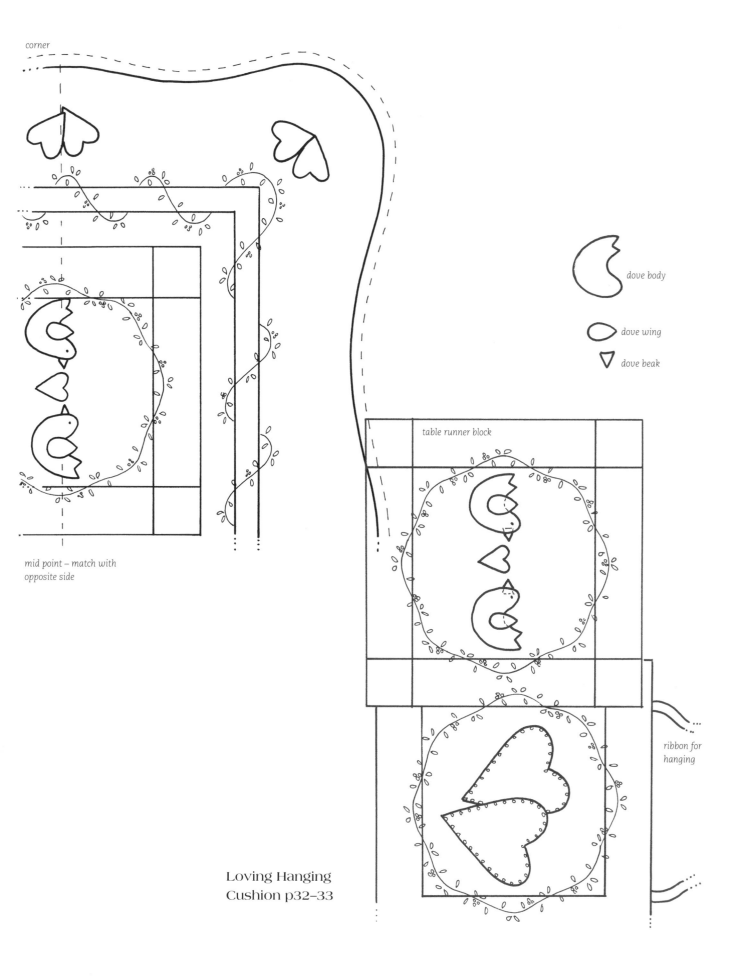

corner

dove body

dove wing

dove beak

mid point – match with
opposite side

table runner block

ribbon for
hanging

Loving Hanging
Cushion p32–33

Tree Decorations p92–93 and Advent Pocket Wallhanging p98–103

Candle Mat and
Birthday Tag p10–11

Hearts and Home
Greeting p68–69 and
Little Cushion p70–72

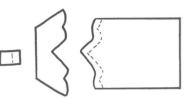

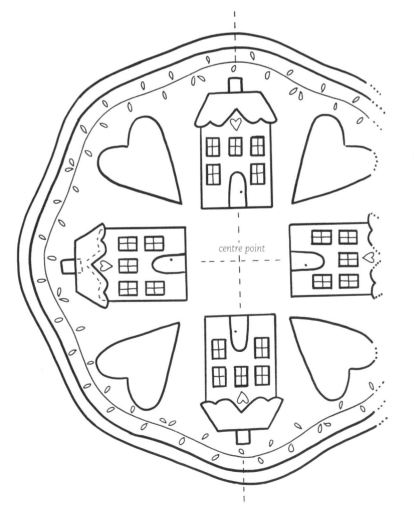

centre point

Candle Mat p69

appliqué view

embroidery view

Little Cushion p73

Birthday Gift Bags p12–15

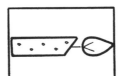

Add pieced border and outer border with French knots with these designs

Christmas Gift Bags p94–97

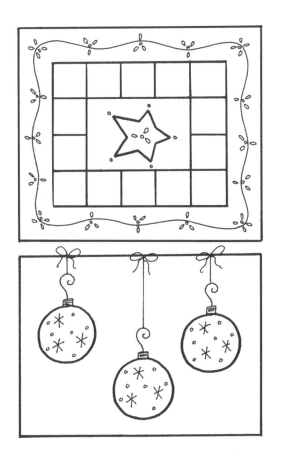

Advent Pocket
Wallhanging p98–103

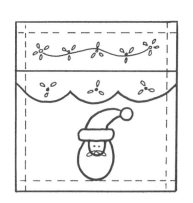

Pocket Carry-All p48–53

pocket E
cut blue background ¼in (6mm) from solid edge for seaming

Cuddly Blanket p44–45
round corner template

Day and Night Cushion p46–47

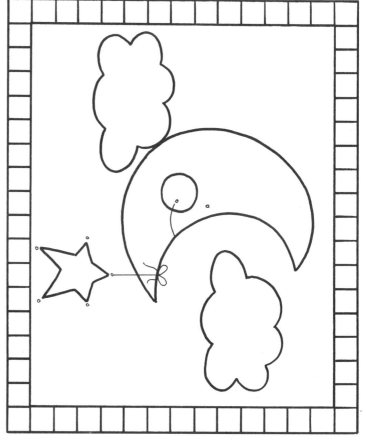

Pocket Carry-All p48–53

pocket F (left side)

Pocket Carry-All layout

*pocket F (right side).
Join two pocket F
designs together to
make a full length*

pocket D

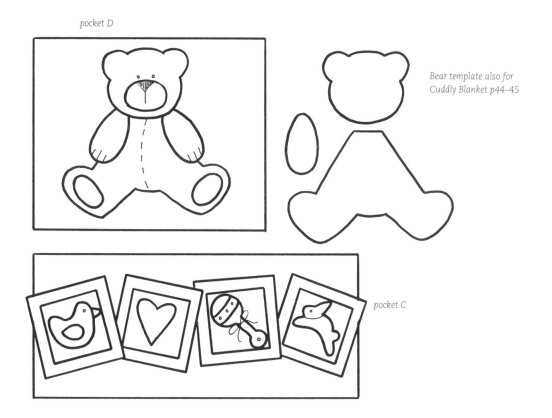

*Bear template also for
Cuddly Blanket p44–45*

pocket C

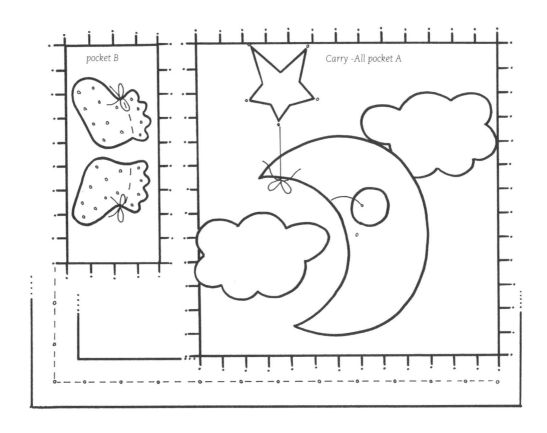

pocket B

Carry -All pocket A

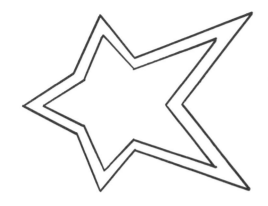

Birthday Garland p16–19

ribbon

*primitive
whipstitch
on applique*

*corner trimmed to
round end*

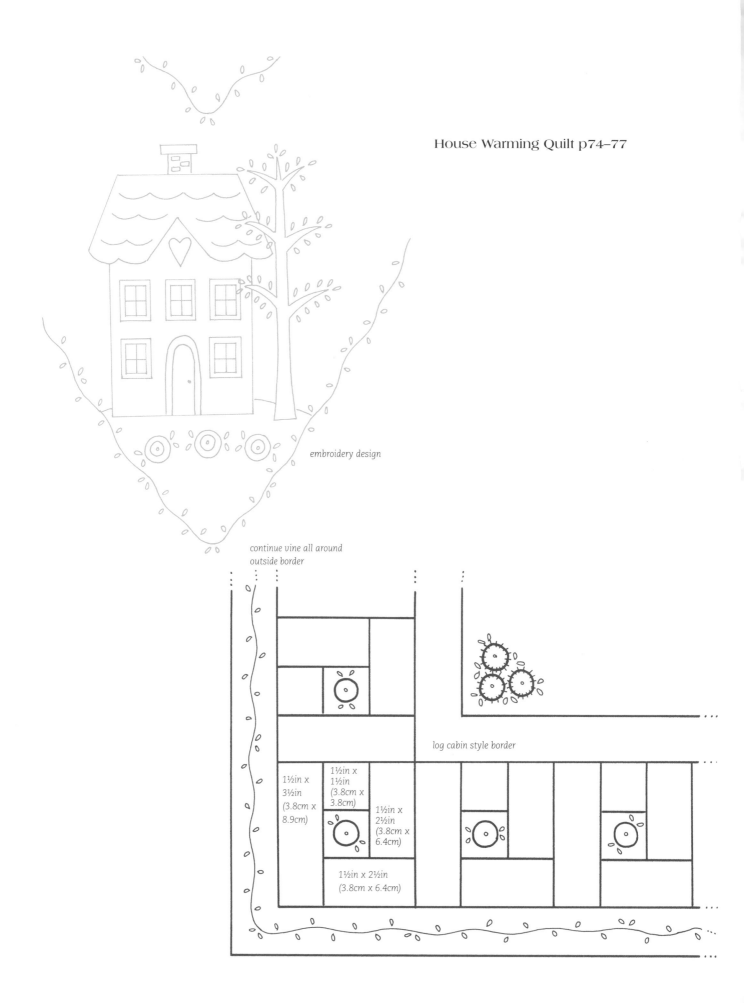

House Warming Quilt p74–77

embroidery design

continue vine all around
outside border

log cabin style border

1½in x
3½in
(3.8cm x
8.9cm)

1½in x
1½in
(3.8cm x
3.8cm)

1½in x
2½in
(3.8cm x
6.4cm)

1½in x 2½in
(3.8cm x 6.4cm)

appliqué design

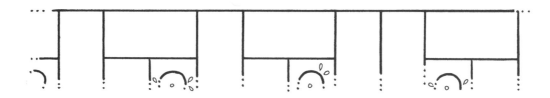

SUPPLIERS

U.K. Suppliers

The Eternal Maker
89 Oving Road
Chichester
West Sussex. PO19 7EW
www.eternalmaker.com
Wool felt, haberdashery, craft fabric.

- - - - - - - - - - - - - - - - - - - -

Whaleys
Harris Court
Great Horton
Bradford, BD7 4EQ
www.whaleys-bradford.ltd.uk
Fabrics, wadding and interfacing.

- - - - - - - - - - - - - - - - - - - -

John Lewis
Draycott Avenue
London SW3 2NA
www.johnlewis.com
Fabrics and haberdashery

U.S. Suppliers

Wool Felt Central
Prairie Point Junction
PO Box 184
Cozad, NE 69130.
(308) 784-2010
prairiepointjunction@yahoo.com
www.woolfeltcentral.com
Cotton fabrics and wool felt.

- - - - - - - - - - - - - - - - - - - -

Homespun Hearth
(866) 346- 0141
www.homespunhearth.com
Fabrics in yards, fat quarters and bundles,
woven wools and wool felt, needlecraft
supplies.

ABOUT THE AUTHOR

Barri Sue Gaudet has been around fabrics and crafts for most of her life. After many years of working in fabric and quilt shops, she began her own pattern company 'Bareroots' in 1999. She has enjoyed creating original designs of all kinds ever since. Barri Sue's designs include little quilts, cushions, and stitcheries and are easily recognized by the delightful elements of nature and sweet little motifs contained in all.

Along with the joy of her work involving what she loves, Barri Sue enjoys the opportunities to teach and meet others who love embroidery.

Barri Sue's other hobbies include knitting, painting, friends and being outdoors.

After raising two sons, Barri Sue moved to a tiny mountain town in the California Sierra Nevada Mountains named June Lake. She lives there with her husband Ron, a dog and two old cats. She has recently opened a stitchery and knitting shop in Bishop, California named, 'Sierra Cottons & Wools'.

Acknowledgements:

From as long as I can remember, in my home my parents always said to my brothers, sister and I, 'you can make that'. I appreciate so much my parents instilling this creative confidence. For my big sister Cheri, thank you so much for guiding and always being there. For my husband Ron and my boys, Eric and Bryce, thank you for all your help, from folding, packing, separating floss, stepping on my pins and needles, to supporting me in every way. For my quilt shops all over the world, thank you for your kind words and encouragement. Thank you Ronnie, for dinners and making me laugh.

INDEX